Steck-Vaughn

English ASAP™

Connecting English to the Workplace

SCANS Consultant

Shirley Brod
Spring Institute for International Studies
Boulder, Colorado

Program Consultants

Judith Dean-Griffin
ESL Teacher
Windham Independent School District
Texas Department of Criminal Justice
Huntsville, Texas

Marilyn K. Spence
Workforce Education Coordinator
Orange Technical Education Centers
Mid-Florida Tech
Orlando, Florida

Brigitte Marshall
English Language Training
for Employment Participation
Albany, California

Dennis Terdy
Director, Community Education
Township High School District 214
Arlington Heights, Illinois

Christine Kay Williams
ESL Specialist
Towson University
Baltimore, Maryland

STECK-VAUGHN®
C O M P A N Y

A Division of Harcourt Brace & Company

Acknowledgments

Executive Editor:	Ellen Northcutt
Supervising Editor:	Tim Collins
Assistant Art Director:	Richard Balsam
Interior Design:	Richard Balsam, Jill Klinger, Paul Durick
Electronic Production:	Jill Klinger, Stephanie Stewart, David Hanshaw, Alan Klemp
Assets Manager:	Margie Foster

Editorial Development: Course Crafters, Inc., Newburyport, Massachusetts

Photo Credits

Alhadeff-p.9, 17b, 17d, 57a, 75; Don Couch Photography-p.25, 33c, 33d, 65, 73; Jack Demuth-p.1; Geno Esponda-p.72; Christine Galida-p.17a, 51, 67; Park Street-p.17c, 15, 57b; Daniel Thompson Photography-p.41.

Illustration Credits

Cover: Tim Dove, D Childress

Cindy Aarvig-p.4b, 11, 12a, 16b-f, 18b, 18e; Meg Aubrey-p.34, 38a, 58, 60; Karl Bailey-p.16a, 18a, 18d; Richard Balsam-p.3, 4a, 7, 12, 23, 64; Chris Celusniak-p.19; David Griffin-p.10a-b, 12c-f, 13; Integrity Graphics/Barbara Beck-p.8, 50, 55, 61, 63b, 66, 71, 72, 74, 76; Laura Jackson-p.18c, 18f; Linda Kelen-p.20, 44, 46, 59, 63a; Kreativ-Designs/Danielle Szabo-p.15, 24, 26, 27, 28, 30-32, 38b, 39, 41, 42, 47, 48, 62; Michael Krone-p.3, 14, 43, 49, 70; Annie Matsick-p.2, 5; John Scott-p.10c-h; Charles Shaw-p.33, 36, 45, 77, 79, 80; Victoria Vebell-p.35, 54.

Contents

To the Student and the Teacher

Every unit of this Workbook has one or more exercises for each section of the Student Book. Use this chart to find the exercise(s) for each section. For example, after the "Talk About It" page, do all the exercises with a 3, such as 3 or 3A, 3B, 3C, etc.

Student Book Section	All Workbook Exercises with the Number
Unit Opener	1
Getting Started	2
Talk About It	3
Keep Talking	4
Listening	5
Grammar	6
Reading and Writing	7
Extension	8
Performance Check	9

Communication

1A. WRITE *YES* OR *NO*

1. He's at work. _____ **yes** _____

2. He's talking on the telephone. _____

3. He's writing a message. _____

4. He's a mail clerk. _____

1B. WRITE THE ANSWERS

1. What do you say when you answer the telephone? _____

2. What's your telephone number at work? At home?

   Work Telephone: _____   Home Telephone: _____

3. Write a telephone number that's important to you. _____

   Whose number is it? _____

4. Write a number you call from work, home, or school. _____

   Whose number is it? _____

2A. WRITE

Complete the sentences.

| call | ~~help~~ | is | May | This |

1. This is Lou. May I _____help_____ you?

2. Maintenance. This _____ Paul.

3. Discount Office Supplies. How may I direct your _____?

4. Hello. Antonio's Restaurant. _____ I help you?

5. _____ is City Dry Cleaners.

2B. ANSWER THE CALL

Write a way that Nadia Petrov can answer the telephone.

_____

_____

2C. WRITE

How do people answer the telephone at your school or at a workplace that you know? What do they say?

_____

Unit 1

3A. WRITE

Look up the telephone numbers in Ruby Lee's Rolodex.

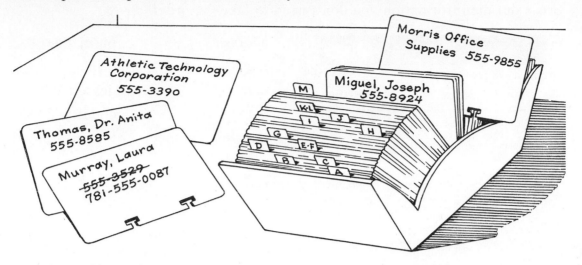

1. What is Dr. Thomas's telephone number? _____**555-8585**_____

2. What is the telephone number for Morris Office Supplies? _____

3. What is Laura Murray's new telephone number? _____

3B. COMPLETE THE DIALOG

Use your name and the numbers from Ruby's Rolodex.

A This is Ruby Lee. May I help you?

B This is _____. Do you know _____'s number?
It's not on my telephone roster.

A _____'s number? Yes, I have it. It's _____.

B Thanks. Bye.

3C. WRITE

Make a Rolodex card for your workplace, your school, or someone you call a lot.

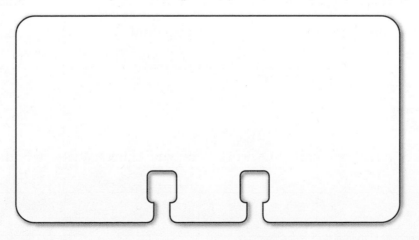

4. TAKING AN ORDER

You work for Pizza House. A customer wants a pizza delivered.
Cross out the information you don't need to take the order.

Pizza Size (check one)

____ small   ____ medium   ____ large

Toppings (check one or more)

____ cheese   ____ green peppers   ____ sausage

____ mushrooms   ____ ham   ____ pepperoni

Caller's Name (write in) _____

Caller's Address (write in) _____

address	pizza size
~~age~~	drink
date	dessert
name	country
telephone number	toppings
time	job

5A. READ AND WRITE

Read the telephone message. Answer the questions.

> Hi, this is Jack Morales in Shipping. It's Thursday at about 10:00. We need some tape and some large paper clips. Can you send us those today? Thanks.

1. Who called? _____ **Jack Morales** _____

2. What time was the call? _____

3. What does Jack want? _____

4. When does he want them? _____

5. Is Jack's message complete? Why do you think so? _____

_____

5B. WRITE

Who makes telephone calls to a workplace you know? Write two ideas.

_____

Unit 1

6A. COMPLETE THE SENTENCES

I'm	in the hall.		You're	in the hall.
He's			We're	
She's			They're	
It's				

1. I work in a factory. I **'m** _____ at work now.

2. This is Carmen. She _____ my coworker.

3. We work five days a week. We _____ full-time workers.

4. Our factory is big. It _____ a computer factory.

6B. WRITE

Complete the sentences.

I	answer the telephone.		He	answers the telephone.
We			She	
You				
They				

1. Samuel ___**opens**___ (**open**) mail.

2. They _____ (**answer**) the telephones.

3. I _____ (**help**) customers.

4. Carlos _____ (**write**) letters.

5. We _____ (**work**) hard.

Unit 1

6C. WRITE THE VERB

Write *have* or *has*.

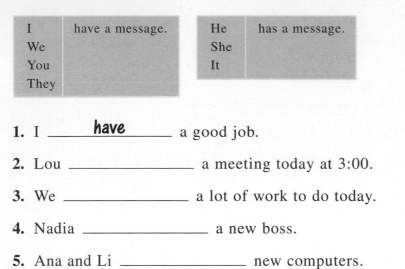

I	have a message.
We	
You	
They	

He	has a message.
She	
It	

1. I _____have_____ a good job.

2. Lou _____ a meeting today at 3:00.

3. We _____ a lot of work to do today.

4. Nadia _____ a new boss.

5. Ana and Li _____ new computers.

6. The fax machine _____ plenty of paper in it.

6D. COMPLETE THE SENTENCES

I	me
he	him
she	her
we	us
you	you
they	them
it	it

Ms. North knows me well.

1. Mrs. Smith is my supervisor at Bright Industries.

   I like _____her_____ (**her/them**).

2. I worked at Bright Industries for ten years.

   Mrs. Smith knows _____ (**her/me**) well.

3. She supervises many workers.

   She knows _____ (**him/them**) well, too.

4. Mr. Smith works at the factory, too.

   I see _____ (**him/us**) with his work team every day.

5. Right now Mr. Smith is in Mrs. Smith's office.

   He's helping _____ (**her/it**).

Unit 1

7. READ AND WRITE

Read the conversation and complete the phone message for Carolina. Use the date and time right now.

A Hello. Human Resources.

B Hi, may I please speak to Carolina?

A Carolina's out of the office. This is Samuel speaking. Can I take a message?

B Yes, Samuel. This is David Salinas in Sales. Can you tell Carolina to call me?

A Sure, what's your extension?

B It's 2990.

A I'll have her call you at 2990 as soon as she gets back.

B Thanks.

For __Carolina_____

Date _____ Time _____

While You Were Out

From _____

Of _____

Phone _____

TELEPHONED		CAME TO SEE YOU	
PLEASE CALL		WILL CALL AGAIN	

MESSAGE _____

_____

_____

_____

SIGNED _____

Susan needs to do the things in the list. Look at the business cards.
Write the name and telephone number of each person Susan needs to call.

1. The copier isn't working. _____ Chen Lee, 555-8962 _____

2. She wants to order lunch for a meeting. _____

3. The office windows need cleaning. _____

9. THINK ABOUT YOUR LEARNING

Check the skills you learned in this unit.

❏ 1. Take telephone messages.

❏ 2. Answer the telephone at work.

❏ 3. Make telephone calls.

❏ 4. Find the telephone numbers I need.

Look at the skills you checked.
Which ones can help you at work? Write the numbers. _____

1A. CIRCLE

Look at the pictures. Circle *yes* or *no*.

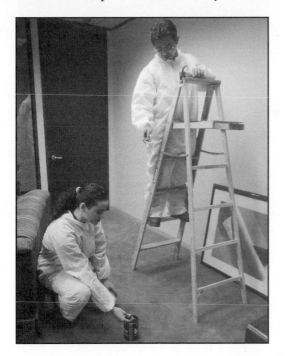 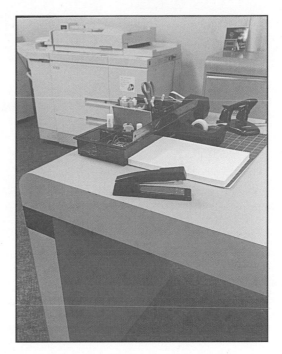

1. Are the workers using a ladder? (yes) no

2. Is there a hand truck in the copy center?   yes   no

3. Is there paper at the copy center?   yes   no

4. Are the workers using a computer?   yes   no

5. Are the workers using a hammer?   yes   no

1B. ANSWER THE QUESTIONS

1. What supplies do you use at work or school? Name five.

_____

_____

2. What do you do when you need supplies?

_____

Write the name of the item.

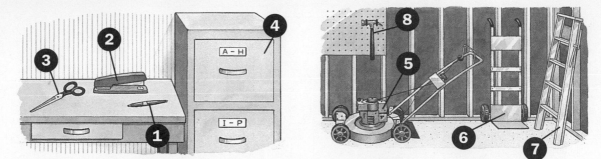

| hammer | file cabinet | hand truck | ladder |
| lawn mower | ~~pen~~ | scissors | stapler |

1. ___pen___   2. _____   3. _____

4. _____   5. _____   6. _____

7. _____   8. _____

2B. WHAT DO YOU NEED?

What do you need to do the work? Write the item from 2A.

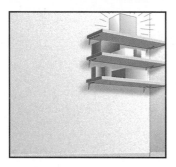   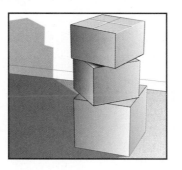   

1. ___ladder___   2. _____   3. _____

COUPON
BLUE RIBBON CAT FOOD
$1.00 OFF

4. _____   5. _____   6. _____

Complete the dialogs. Use the words in the box.

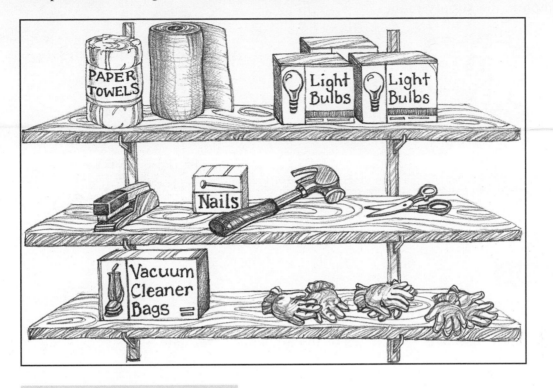

top	bottom	middle

1. **A** Where are the paper towels?

   B They're on the _____ **top** _____ shelf.

2. **A** Where's the hammer?

   B It's on the _____ shelf.

3. **A** Where are the vacuum cleaner bags?

   B They're on the _____ shelf.

4. **A** Where are the gloves?

   B They're on the _____ shelf.

5. **A** Where are the nails?

   B They're on the _____ shelf.

6. **A** Where are the light bulbs?

   B They're on the _____ shelf.

7. **A** Where's the stapler?

   B It's on the _____ shelf.

4. WRITE

Look at the picture. What supplies does Ms. Block need?
Complete the supply request.

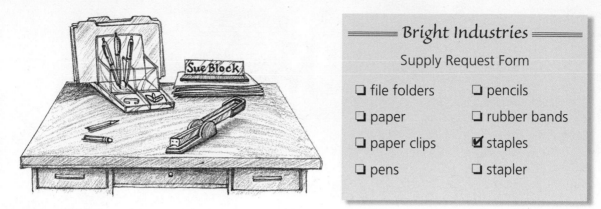

Bright Industries
Supply Request Form

❏ file folders   ❏ pencils

❏ paper   ❏ rubber bands

❏ paper clips   ☑ staples

❏ pens   ❏ stapler

5. WRITE

Look at the pictures. How are the things organized? Write the letter.

a. number   **b.** size   **c.** letter of the alphabet   ~~**d.**~~ date

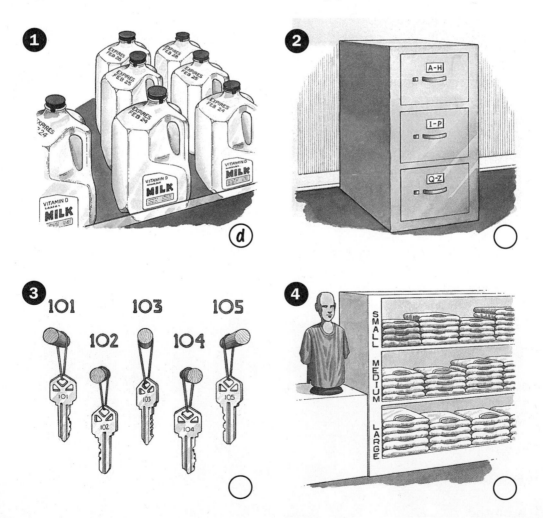

1. _d_

2. ◯

3. ◯

4. ◯

| Is | there | a bulletin board? | Yes, there | is. | No, there | isn't. |
| Are | | staples in the stapler? | | are. | | aren't. |

1. **A** ___Are there___ light bulbs?

    B ___Yes, there are.___

2. **A** _____ a ladder?

    B _____

3. **A** _____ bulletin boards?

    B _____

4. **A** _____ a lawn mower?

    B _____

5. **A** _____ a cart?

    B _____

6. **A** _____ rubber bands?

    B _____

7. **A** _____ a hammer?

    B _____

8. **A** _____ a copier?

    B _____

6B. WRITE

Complete the sentences.

| Do you need any | file folders? | Yes, I need some. | No, I don't need any. |
| | paper? | | |

A Do you need ___any___ file folders from the supply room?

B Yes, I need _____ file folders. I need _____ rubber bands, too.

A Do you need _____ paper or tape?

B I need _____ paper, but I don't need _____ tape.

Unit 2

Look at the picture. Complete the sentences.

There's a ladder	against	the truck.
	behind	
	inside	
	on top of	
	under	
	on	
	over	

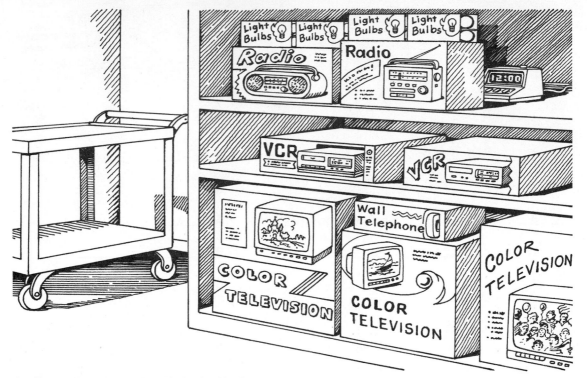

1. **A** Where are the light bulbs?

   B They're _____on top of_____ (**on top of/inside**) the radios.

2. **A** Where are the TVs?

   B They're _____ (**under/over**) the VCRs.

3. **A** Where's the telephone?

   B It's _____ (**inside/on top of**) a television.

4. **A** Where's the clock?

   B It's _____ (**against/behind**) a radio.

5. **A** Where's the cart?

   B It's _____ (**inside/against**) the wall.

Unit 2

7A. WRITE

Which papers should go in each file folder? Write the letters on the file folders.

a. electricity bills
c. your resume
e. instructions for an electric pencil sharpener
g. bills for food from the company picnic

b. the manual for an electric stapler
d. telephone bills
f. the directions for a new dishwasher

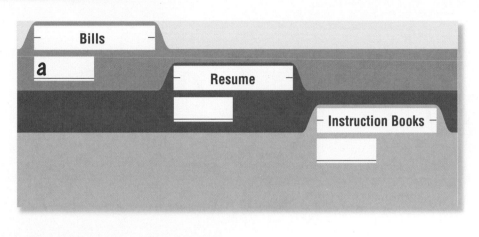

7B. READ LAURA'S PAPERS

Laura needs files for these papers. What should she name the files? Write the file names on the file folders.

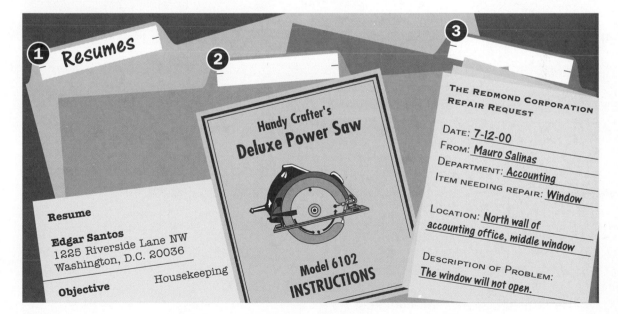

Look at the pictures. What do you do with each thing? Write the letter.

a. I wash them with soap and water.

~~b.~~ I fill it with gas.

c. I put in staples.

d. I order more when the supply is low.

e. I put in paper.

f. I put air in the tires.

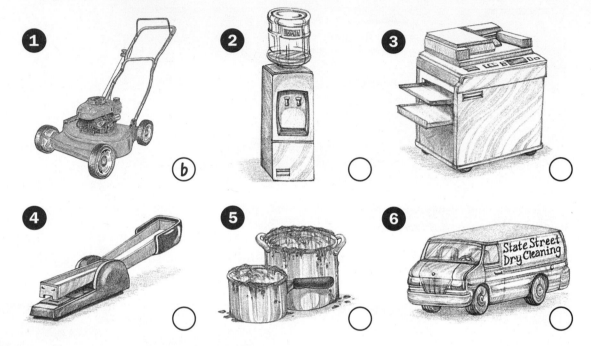

9. THINK ABOUT YOUR LEARNING

Check the skills you learned in this unit.

❏ 1. Get the supplies I need.

❏ 2. Organize materials.

❏ 3. Maintain supplies and equipment.

❏ 4. Use file systems.

Look at the skills you checked.
Which ones can help you at work? Write the numbers. _____

Technology

1A. MATCH

Look at the pictures. What are the people doing? Write the letter.

a. She's putting oil in the van.

b. He's repairing the vacuum cleaner.

c. He's cleaning the computer screen.

d. He's fixing the copier.

1B. WRITE

What machines do you take care of at your workplace, school, or home?

Write three. _____

Unit 3

2A. WRITE

Write the name of the item. Use the words in the box.

| cash register | lawn mower | microwave oven | oil | ~~tire~~ | van |

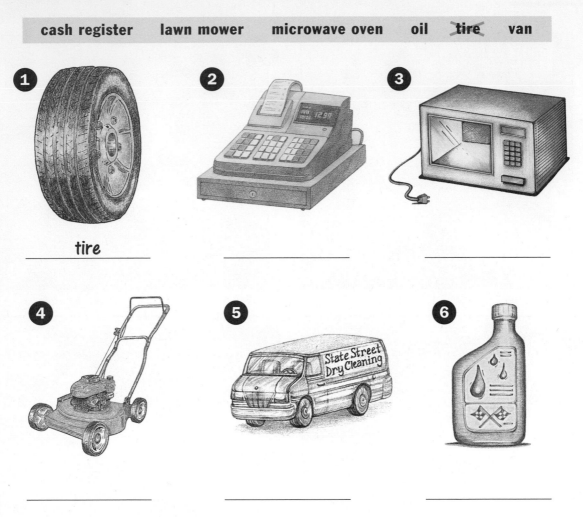

1

tire

2

3

4

5

6

2B. CIRCLE THE ANSWER

1. Do you know how to clean a microwave oven?   yes   no

2. Do you know how to put gas in a lawn mower?   yes   no

3. Do you know how to check the tires on a car?   yes   no

4. Do you know how to put tape in a cash register?   yes   no

5. Do you know how to put oil in a van?   yes   no

2C. WRITE

Think of a machine you can take care of. What can you do? Write a sentence.

I can change the tires of a car.

Unit 3

3A. COMPLETE THE DIALOG

ask   broken   department   fix   say   maintenance

A The ice maker is _____ broken _____ .

B Did you _____ Bill for help?

He can usually _____ it.

A Yes, I did. He told me to call the maintenance _____ .

B What did they _____ ?

A They told me to fill out a _____ request.

3B. ANSWER THE QUESTIONS

Answer the questions about your workplace or school.

1. What machines can you fix?

_____

2. What machines can't you fix?

_____

3. A toilet is broken. What do you do?

_____

Unit 3

4. WRITE

Look at the pictures. What did the people do wrong? Write a sentence.

1. _____ He put his coffee on the computer. _____

2. _____

3. _____

4. _____

5. READ AND WRITE

Read the maintenance report. Answer the questions.

1. What is the date of the report?

   _____ October 25 _____

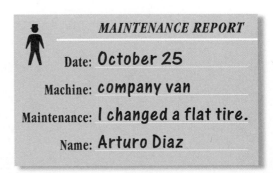

MAINTENANCE REPORT

Date: **October 25**

Machine: **company van**

Maintenance: **I changed a flat tire.**

Name: **Arturo Diaz**

2. What needed maintenance?

   _____

3. What maintenance was done?

   _____

4. Who did the work?

   _____

Unit 3

6A. COMPLETE THE SENTENCES

I	cleaned	the machine.
He	didn't clean	
She		
It		
We		
You		
They		

1. We _____fixed_____ (**fix**) the flat tire on the truck.

2. Ana _____ (**not clean**) the refrigerator.

3. Diane _____ (**check**) the coffee maker.

4. Anita _____ (**not sharpen**) the knife.

5. They _____ (**not change**) the oil in the van.

6B. WRITE SENTENCES

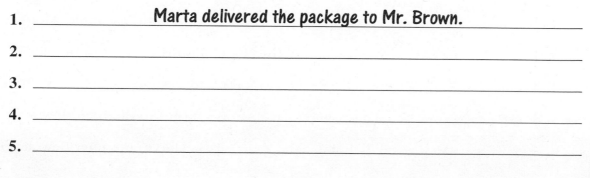

My To-Do List

✔ 1. Deliver the package to Mr. Brown.

2. Help Joyce organize the supply room.

✔ 3. Clean the kitchen in the break room.

4. Repair the cash register.

5. Fix the coffee maker.

Read Marta's to-do list. What did she do? What didn't she do?
(A ✔ means she did it.)

1. _____Marta delivered the package to Mr. Brown._____

2. _____

3. _____

4. _____

5. _____

Unit 3

6C. COMPLETE THE DIALOG

Did	I	fix the faucet?
	you	
	he	
	she	
	we	
	they	

Yes,	I	did.
No,		didn't.

A _____Did_____ you _____work_____ (**work**) late last night?

B No, I didn't. I _____finished_____ (**finish**) the big project at 4:00.

A _____ you _____ (**like**) the project?

B Yes, I _____ . I _____ (**like**) it a lot.

A _____ you _____ (**start**) a new project today?

B Yes, I _____ . I _____ (**start**) it first thing this morning.

A _____ you _____ (**talk**) to Ms. Smith about the project?

B No, I _____ . I _____ (**talk**) to Mr. Lee about the project.

6D. WRITE

Complete the sentences.

I	went	to the meeting.
	didn't go	

Irregular Verbs	
bring	brought
buy	bought
go	went
have	had
make	made
send	sent
take	took

1. I _____sent_____ (**send**) an application letter to Bright Industries.

2. I _____ (**not sent**) an application form.

3. I _____ (**buy**) a new shirt to wear to the interview.

4. I _____ (**take**) my resume to the job interview.

5. I _____ (**go**) to the interview at 2:00.

6. I _____ (**have**) the interview at 3:00.

Unit 3

Choose the repair code. Write it on the service request.

VALLEY HOTEL
SERVICE REQUEST

Name: Kim Lee

Date: March 17

Equipment: lamp

Description: The floor lamp in room 122 doesn't work. The switch is broken.

For service technician only: SERVICE CODE

VALLEY HOTEL
SERVICE REQUEST

Name: Joel Prevalus

Date: March 28

Equipment: carpet

Description: The carpet in room 111 has a large worn spot in front of the door. It needs to be replaced.

For service technician only: SERVICE CODE

VALLEY HOTEL
REPAIR CODES

Service Requests

Call an electrician	009
Call a plumber	011
Order new furniture	018
Order new carpeting	052
Call Housekeeping	073

7B. WRITE

The clock in the break room doesn't work. Write a service request.
Use your name and today's date.

VALLEY HOTEL
SERVICE REQUEST

Name:

Date:

Equipment:

Description:

8. READ THE USER'S MANUAL

Read the manual and the sentences. Which directions did the people follow?
Write the letter.

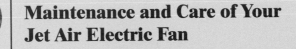

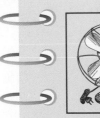

**Maintenance and Care of Your
Jet Air Electric Fan**

a.   The fan should have at least 18 inches of space all around it.

b.   Set the fan on a wide, steady surface.

c.   The cord should be against the wall.

d.   Don't put liquids on or near the fan.

e.   Keep hair, jewelry, clothing, and papers away from the fan.

f.   Do not insert anything into the moving fan.

g.   Keep children away from the fan.

1. Donna put the fan on a large, strong table. __*b*__

2. Mary left plenty of space all around the fan. _____

3. Brian didn't put his coffee near the fan. _____

4. Sam put the cord against the wall. _____

5. Ana's children didn't play near the fan. _____

9. THINK ABOUT YOUR LEARNING

Check the skills you learned in this unit.

❏ 1. Complete a maintenance request.

❏ 2. Talk about problems with machines.

❏ 3. Read a user's manual.

Look at the skills you checked.
Which ones can help you at work? Write the numbers. _____

Unit 3

1A. ANSWER THE QUESTIONS

Look at the picture. Read the sentences. Circle *yes* or *no*.

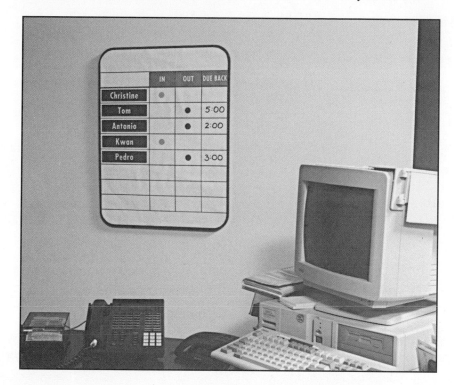

	IN	OUT	DUE BACK
Christine	●		
Tom		●	5:00
Antonio		●	2:00
Kwan	●		
Pedro		●	3:00

1. Two employees are in the office.   (yes)   no
2. Tom is in the office.   yes   no
3. Antonio will be in the office at 2:00.   yes   no
4. Kwan is out of the office.   yes   no
5. Pedro will be in the office at 3:00.   yes   no

1B. WRITE

1. Do you have schedules at work or school? What information is on them?

   _____

2. Does your workplace or school have a holiday schedule? Where is it?

   _____

3. Do you have a calendar at home? What do you write on it?

   _____

2A. WRITE

City Computer Company wants to have a meeting at the Park Hotel.
Complete the dialog. Use the words in the box.

about	free	How	~~meeting~~	sorry

A Hello, Park Hotel.

B Hi, I want to set up a _____meeting_____ for 30 people on July 15.

A July 15. I'm _____. Our meeting room isn't free that day.

   How _____ July 16?

B No, that won't work. _____ about July 14?

A July 14? That's good. Our meeting room is _____ that day.
   What time's your meeting?

B It's from 10:00 to 4:00.

2B. WRITE

Look at 2A. Write City Computer Company's meeting on the schedule.

Meeting Room Schedule, July 12–18

Sunday	Monday	Tuesday	Wednesday	Thursday	Friday	Saturday
12	13	14	15	16	17	18
Hotel Staff Meeting 6:00			Smith Vacuum Cleaner Co. 8:00-5:00		Best Industries 9:00-4:00	Best Industries 9:00-3:00

2C. WRITE

Big Mountain Skis wants to have a meeting from 9:00 to 7:00 at the Park Hotel.
They want to have it the week of July 12 to 18. They don't want to meet
on Monday. When can they have the meeting? Write it on the calendar.

3. READ

Read the schedule. Answer the questions.

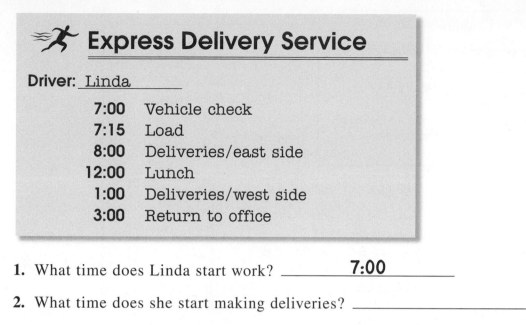

1. What time does Linda start work? _____ **7:00** _____

2. What time does she start making deliveries? _____

3. Can she deliver a package to the west side in the morning? _____

4. Can she deliver a package to the east side in the morning? _____

4. READ AND WRITE

Read the ad. Answer the questions.

1. What day is the sale? _____ **Thursday, May 14** _____

2. What time does the store open? _____

3. It's 11:00. Can customers save 50% on watches? ___ _____

4. It's 2:00. Can customers get free coffee and cake? _____

Read the meeting requests. Answer the questions.

The Grand Garden Hotel

Set-up request for room: **Lake Room**
Date of meeting: **January 23**
Time of meeting: **9:00 a.m.-11:00 a.m.**
Number of chairs: **200**
Number of tables: **4 (at entry, for name tags and brochures)**

The Grand Garden Hotel

Set-up request for room: **Meeting Room 1**
Date of meeting: **January 23**
Time of meeting: **9:30 a.m.-noon**
Number of chairs: **60**
Number of tables: **6**

The Grand Garden Hotel

Set-up request for room: **Grand Ballroom**
Date of meeting: **January 23**
Time of meeting: **6:00 p.m.-9:00 p.m.**
Number of chairs: **350**
Number of tables: **5**

1. How many chairs are needed in the Lake Room? _____200_____

2. What day are the meetings? _____

3. What time does the meeting in Meeting Room 1 begin? _____

4. When does the meeting in the Grand Ballroom end? _____

5. How many tables are needed in the Grand Ballroom? _____

Read the sentences below. When can Shelly see the people?
Write the times on her schedule.

▬ ▬ Shelly's Plumbing ▬ ▬

9:00 _____
10:00 _____
11:00 _Sunja Kim_____
12:00 _____

1. Tim Young needs Shelly to come early so he can get to work.
2. Donna Diaz wants Shelly to come between 11:45 and 12:45.
3. Diane Johnson wants Shelly to come to her house at 11:00 or earlier.

Unit 4

Write sentences. Use *have to* or *has to* and the words below.

I	have to	deliver these packages.
We	don't have to	
You		
They		
He	has to	
She	doesn't have to	

1. (you/punch in)

   _____ You have to punch in. _____

2. (they/go to meetings)

   _____

3. (we/not work on weekends)

   _____

4. (she/work with a team)

   _____

5. (he/not wear a uniform)

   _____

Do	I	have to sign the attendance sheet?
	we	
	you	
	they	
Does	he	
	she	

A _____ Do _____ we _____ have to clean _____ (**clean**) the microwave oven?

B Yes, we _____ (**clean**) it every day.

A _____ we _____ (**wash**) the towels now?

B No, we _____ (**not wash**) them now.

We _____ (**wash**) them this afternoon.

A _____ we _____ (**make**) the beds?

B Yes, we _____ (**make**) them every morning.

Unit 4

I'm We're You're They're	going to be late.	He's She's It's	going to be late.	When Why	are you going to do it?

Wednesday, March 20
Pedro Martinez

8:30 to 9:00	Sort overnight packages
9:00 to 10:00	Deliver packages to departments
10:00 to 11:00	Prepare outgoing packages
12:00 to 1:00	Lunch
1:00 to 2:00	Sort mail
2:00 to 4:00	Deliver mail

What's Pedro going to do tomorrow? Write sentences.

1. _____ He's going to sort overnight packages from 8:30 to 9:00. _____

2. _____

3. _____

4. _____

Complete the sentences. Use *going to*.

1. I _____ .

2. I _____ .

3. I'm not _____ .

4. My boss _____ .

5. My coworkers _____ .

30

Unit 4

7A. READ

Read Aura's tasks for the day. Help her organize her work. Circle the tasks she will do at the mall. Underline the tasks she will do at the warehouse.

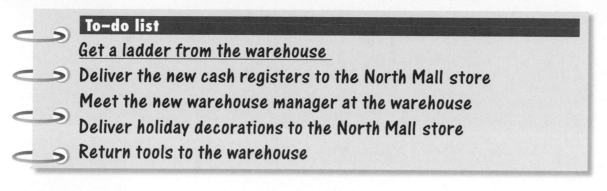

To-do list

<u>Get a ladder from the warehouse</u>

Deliver the new cash registers to the North Mall store

Meet the new warehouse manager at the warehouse

Deliver holiday decorations to the North Mall store

Return tools to the warehouse

7B. WRITE

Read the sentences below. Then fill in Lin's calendar.

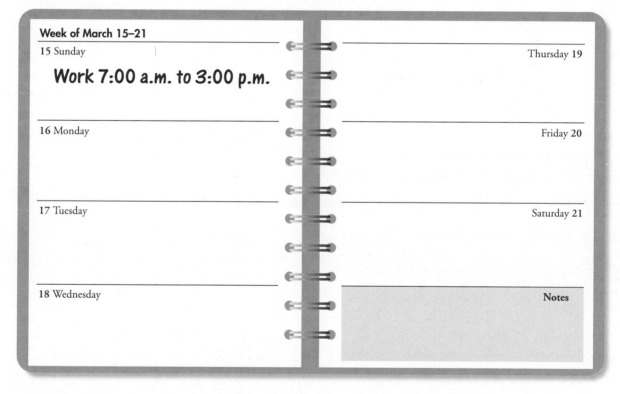

Week of March 15–21

15 Sunday

Work 7:00 a.m. to 3:00 p.m.

16 Monday

17 Tuesday

18 Wednesday

Thursday 19

Friday 20

Saturday 21

Notes

1. He has to work from 7:00 AM. to 3:00 PM. on Sunday, Monday, Tuesday, and Wednesday.

2. He has an appointment with the dentist at 2:00 PM. on Thursday. It will take one hour.

3. He has an English class from 7:00 PM. to 9:00 PM. on Tuesday and Thursday.

4. He has a job interview on Friday from 9:00 AM. to 10:00 AM.

5. He's going to go to the movies with his friends on Friday at 6:00 PM.

Unit 4

8. READ AND WRITE

Look at the holiday schedule. Answer the questions.

Green Street Restaurant
Holiday Hours

Wednesday, November 27	11:30 AM to 3:00 PM
Thursday, November 28	Closed
Friday, November 29	11:30 AM to 11:30 PM

1. Is the restaurant open on November 27 for lunch? _____ *yes* _____

2. Is the restaurant open on November 27 for dinner? _____

3. What day is the restaurant closed? _____

4. What time does the restaurant open on November 29? _____

9. THINK ABOUT YOUR LEARNING

Check the skills you learned in this unit.

❏ 1. Understand schedules.

❏ 2. Interpret a holiday schedule.

❏ 3. Use calendars and planners.

Look at the skills you checked.
Which ones can help you at work? Write the numbers. _____

Unit 4

Customer Service

1 ⓒ

2 ◯

3 ◯

4 ◯

1A. LOOK AND MATCH

Look at the pictures. What requests are the people making? Write the letter.

a. We'd like a taxi, please.

b. I'd like the hamburger special without onions, please.

c. Where's the soap?

d. Could you put the bush over here?

1B. WRITE

What kind of requests do you make or hear in workplaces? Write three.

1. _____

2. _____

3. _____

2A. WRITE

Complete the dialog. Use the words in the box.

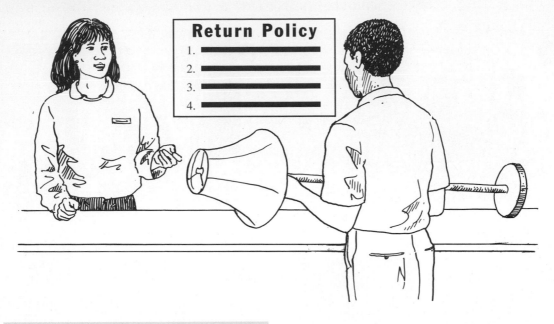

| credit | ~~refund~~ | show | Can |

A Can I get a cash _____refund_____ for this floor lamp?

B I'm sorry. We only give store _____.

A _____ I get a table lamp instead?

B Yes, let me _____ you what we have.

2B. WRITE A RESPONSE

Write what you would say in each situation.

1. A customer asks for a discount price. (no)

   _____**I'm sorry. I need to check that with my supervisor.**_____

2. Your manager asks you to help with a small project. (yes)

   _____

3. Your coworker asks you to work her Saturday shift. (no)

   _____

4. A customer asks you to carry a heavy package. (yes)

   _____

Unit 5

3A. WRITE

Look at the picture. There are too many bags for the taxi. What can the bellhop and taxi driver do? Complete their suggestions. Then write your own suggestion.

Why don't . . . ?   Let's . . . .   Why not . . . ?

1. _____**Why don't**_____ you take two cabs?

2. _____ put some bags on the roof.

3. _____ put some bags in the front seat?

4. _____

3B. WRITE

Think of a customer service problem at your school or workplace. Think of two suggestions that will fix the problem. Write your ideas.

Problem:

_____

My ideas:

1. _____

2. _____

4. MATCH

Match the customer's request and the employee's response.

1 ⓒ

I don't want any ice in my drink.

2 ◯

Can you make these copies in ten minutes?

3 ◯

Excuse me, I need some help with my suitcases.

4 ◯

Can you make sure these glasses won't break when I mail them?

a. Sorry, it will take at least thirty minutes.
b. Of course. I'll put extra paper around them.
c. OK, that's one orange soda with no ice.
d. No problem. I'll carry them for you.

5. CIRCLE

Where does the dialog take place?

1. A Could you get me a notebook from the supply room?
   B Sure, I can run down to the supply room in a few minutes.

   (an office)   a city street

2. A Take me to the central bus station, please. How far is that?
   B It's about two miles. We'll be there in five minutes.

   a taxi   a restaurant

3. A Put a "No Parking" sign in front of the building we're painting.
   B Sure, where are the signs?

   a city street   a bus

Unit 5

Where	did you	buy this machine?
When		call the service center?
How		fix it?

I	bought it at the downtown store.
	called last week.
	fixed it with a new part.

Irregular Verbs	
buy	bought
do	did
find	found
get	got
make	made
pay	paid
see	saw
tell	told
wear	wore

Complete the conversations. Write *where*, *when*, or *how*.
Write the correct form of the verb.

1. A _____Where_____ did you buy that desk?

B I _____bought_____ (**buy**) it at the mall.

2. A _____ did you see Mr. Miller?

B I _____ (**see**) him last week.

3. A _____ did Carlos find a job?

B He _____ (**find**) a job at Perfect Painting Company.

4. A _____ did you get to work yesterday?

B I _____ (**get**) to work by bus.

5. A _____ did Pablo make the copies?

B He _____ (**make**) them this morning.

6B. WRITE

A friend started a new job last week. What did he or she do? Write 3 questions.

_____How did you get to work?_____

_____

_____

_____

Write the words to complete each sentence.

Did	you	help the customer?
	he	

Yes,	I	did.
No,		didn't.

A _____Did_____ Luis _____check_____ (**check**) the engine?

B Yes, he _____did_____.

A _____ he _____ (**check**) the oil?

B Yes, he _____.

A _____ he _____ (**change**) only one headlight?

B No, he _____. He changed both headlights.

A _____ he _____ (**change**) the tires?

B Yes, he _____.

A _____ he _____ (**put**) gas in the car?

B No, he _____.

Read the Return Policy. Then read about the customers and about the Ticket Center employee, Nina, on page 39. Did Nina follow the policy? Write *yes* or *no*.

THE TICKET CENTER ◤

Tickets cannot be returned, exchanged, or refunded except when a show is canceled.

When a show is canceled, tickets may be returned for a refund.

Refunds are made by check. There are NO CASH REFUNDS.
For a refund, customers must bring their tickets to The Ticket Center.

<u>yes</u> **1.** Pedro Salinas wanted to return his tickets. The concert wasn't cancelled. Nina said that there were no returns.

_____ **2.** Carlos Diaz had to work on the night of his concert. He wanted to exchange his ticket for a different concert. Nina exchanged the ticket.

_____ **3.** A concert was canceled. Sunja Li brought her tickets to the Ticket Center and asked for a refund. Nina gave her a refund.

_____ **4.** A show was canceled. Joyce Johnson called on the telephone. She wanted a refund. Nina told her to bring her tickets to the Ticket Center.

_____ **5.** Marty Clarke bought a ticket to a concert. Nina told him that tickets cannot be returned except when a show is cancelled.

7B. WRITE

You work at the Ticket Center. Complete the refund form for Joyce Johnson. She had two tickets to the Brown Sisters' Concert at City Stadium on May 7. The tickets cost $15 each. Her address is 3990 E. Byfield Road, Houston, Texas 75103.

THE TICKET CENTER

Ticket Exchange Form

Tickets for: <u>**The Brown Sisters at City Stadium**</u> on <u>**May 7**</u>

Tickets: Number_____ Price $_____ Total $_____

Customer's Name: _____

Customer's Mailing Address:_____

_____

_____

Employee Signature _____ Date _____

8. READ

What would you say? Choose your response.

1. You work in a bakery. A woman wants to try something before she places a very large order.

    a. I'm sorry. We don't give people free food.

    (b.) Sure, I'll cut you a piece.

2. An angry customer wants to talk to your manager immediately. The customer will not tell you the reason.

    a. I'll get the manager right away.

    b. If you don't tell me the problem, I can't help you. Goodbye.

3. You work in a restaurant. A customer calls on the telephone. She thinks she left her wallet in the restaurant. She wants you to search her table, the ladies' room, and the floor.

    a. Please give me your telephone number. I'll call you back after we check.

    b. I'll look for it during my break and call you back. What's your telephone number?

4. A customer wants a lot of photocopies in 1 hour. You know the job will take 2 hours.

    a. I'll have them ready in an hour.

    b. This is a big job. I can give you half the copies in 1 hour and the others in 2 hours.

9. THINK ABOUT YOUR LEARNING

Check the skills you learned in this unit.

❏ 1. Respond to requests.

❏ 2. Handle special requests.

❏ 3. Offer suggestions.

❏ 4. Understand customer service policies.

Look at the skills you checked.
Which ones can help you at work? Write the numbers. _____

Unit 5

UNIT 6 — Culture of Work

Fresh Foods, Inc.

Employee of the Month:
Angela Simms

Congratulations to Angela Simms this month's

1A. CIRCLE

Why do you think Angela is the Employee of the Month? Circle the numbers.

1. She always gets to work on time.

2. She does a good job.

3. She's absent a lot.

4. She works well with others.

5. She's very helpful to customers

6. She never says, "Thank you."

1B. WRITE

Write three more reasons why a person might win the Employee of the Month Award.

1. _____

2. _____

3. _____

2A. MATCH

Read the notice from Best Department Store. Then read the reason for each policy. Match the policy and the reason. Write the letter.

Best Department Store

The following company policies have been established for all Best Department Store employees

a. Workers have to park in the employee lot behind the store.
b. Workers have to say "Hello" to each customer.
c. Workers have to be at their work stations 10 minutes before the store opens.

_c_ **1.** The store needs to be ready for customers when it opens.

_____ **2.** Best Department Store wants customers to have room to park in front of the store.

_____ **3.** Customers should feel good about shopping at Best Department Store.

2B. CIRCLE OR WRITE

What is the policy at your school or workplace?
Circle an answer or write your own.

1. Getting supplies

   a. Workers can check out supplies.

   b. One worker gives out all supplies.

   c. _____

2. Parking

   a. Workers can park anywhere.

   b. Workers have to park in the employee lot.

   c. _____

3. Being on time

   a. Workers can be a few minutes late.

   b. Workers should be on time.

   c. _____

4. Smoking

   a. There is no smoking at work.

   b. Workers can smoke in certain areas.

   c. _____

Unit 6

3A. WRITE

Look at the picture. Complete the dialog.

| Can | can't | ~~Excuse~~ | idea | off | sorry |

A ___Excuse___ me, Rick. _____ you work for me on Wednesday?

B I'm _____, Sylvia. I'm busy on Wednesday.

A What can I do? I _____ come in on Wednesday.

B Why don't you ask Edgar? He has Wednesday _____.

A Thanks. That's a good _____.

3B. WRITE

Your boss wants you to work tomorrow from 11:00 to 6:00. You have a doctor's appointment at 3:00. What do you tell your boss? Offer two compromises.

1. I can _____.

2. I could _____.

4A. MATCH

Look at the pictures. Read the requests. Match the request and the picture.

a. Excuse me. Are these your papers and tools? Could you please clean up this area?

b. It's getting late, and we need to move this box. Can you call that person back later?

c. Excuse me. It's a little bit loud at my desk. Could you talk somewhere else?

4B. WRITE

Look at the picture. What can she say? Write a polite request.

_____

_____

5A. CHECK

Anita is a dressmaker. Check the good work habits that you see.

- ❏ She's rarely absent.
- ❏ She gets to work on time.
- ❏ She does good work.
- ❏ She works hard.
- ❏ She's helpful to others.
- ❏ She's friendly.
- ❏ She's honest.
- ❏ She's cooperative.
- ❏ She's very careful.
- ❏ She follows the safety rules.
- ❏ She learns new things quickly.
- ❏ She finishes work on time.

5B. THINK AND WRITE

What are your good work habits?

_____

_____

Unit 6

Al is a bus driver. He needs a new uniform. Complete the sentences.

The new trucks are	faster	than the old ones.
	bigger	
	heavier	
	nicer	
	better	
	worse	

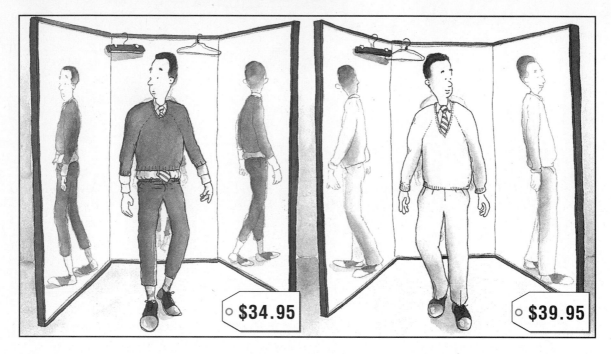

1. The gray uniform is _____smaller than_____ (**small**) the white uniform.

2. The white uniform is _____ (**large**) the gray uniform.

3. The white sweater is _____ (**big**) the gray sweater.

4. The white pants are _____ (**long**) the gray pants.

5. The gray uniform is _____ (**cheap**) the white uniform.

6. The gray uniform is _____ (**ugly**) the white uniform.

7. The white uniform is _____ (**nice**) the gray uniform.

8. The gray uniform is _____ (**bad**) the white uniform.

9. The gray pants are _____ (**tight**) the white pants.

10. The white uniform is _____ (**good**) the gray uniform.

Unit 6

Look at the uniforms on page 46. Complete the sentences.

This shirt is	more expensive than more comfortable than	that shirt.

1. The gray sweater is <u>more practical than</u> (**practical**) the white sweater.

2. The white uniform is _____ (**expensive**) the gray uniform.

3. The white pants are _____ (**comfortable**) the gray pants.

4. The white uniform is _____ (**attractive**) the gray uniform.

Read the company rules for Southwest Car Rental.
Circle *yes* or *no* for each employee's request.

Southwest Car Rental

Company Rules

1. Employees may not make or receive personal phone calls during their work hours, except in emergency situations.

2. Employees may not drive company cars for personal use.

3. Employees may not smoke on company property.

4. Employees have to wear their uniforms every day.

1. Brian wants to drive a company car to a restaurant to eat lunch.   yes   (no)

2. Ron doesn't like his uniform pants. He wants to wear jeans.   yes   no

3. Rick wants to call his girlfriend.   yes   no

4. Caroline wants to smoke in the break room.   yes   no

5. Amanda's daughter had an accident at school. The school left a message for Amanda. Amanda wants to call the school back.   yes   no

You are the manager at the Luxury Inn's child care center. Sometimes child care aides arrive late or leave early. Sometimes they don't clean up at the end of the day. Write policies to correct the problems.

Child care aides have to arrive on time.

_____

_____

8. WRITE

Read the mission statement for Hamburgers and More.
Circle the company's goals below.

serve good food   have low prices

serve food fast   serve large hamburgers

9. THINK ABOUT YOUR LEARNING

Check the skills you learned in this unit.

❑ **1.** Follow rules.

❑ **2.** Make compromises.

❑ **3.** Understand company policies and goals.

❑ **4.** Get along with others.

Look at the skills you checked.
Which ones can help you at work? Write the numbers. _____

Finances

1A. CIRCLE

Look at the picture. Read the questions. Circle the answer.

1. Where is the man?

   (in a library)   in a bookstore   in a bank

2. What is he doing?

   getting a book   getting tax forms   getting paid

3. What do people use tax forms for?

   to pay taxes   to get their paychecks   to get new jobs

1B. WRITE

Answer the questions.

1. When are you paid?

_____

2. Where do you get tax forms?

_____

3. Do you think your taxes are high or low? Why do you think so?

_____

2A. CIRCLE

Look at Guy Matesa's paycheck. Answer the questions.

Green River Parks Department

NAME: Guy Matesa

SOCIAL SECURITY NUMBER: 000-99-8066

CHECK NUMBER: 56560

RATE	HOURS	EARNINGS	YEAR TO DATE
$11.00	80.00	$880.00	$12,215.00

GROSS PAY $880.00
PAY PERIOD BEGINNING   09-01-99
PAY PERIOD ENDING   09-15-99

DEDUCTIONS	
Federal tax	$104.15
State tax	$65.20
FICA	$38.50
Medicare	$7.20
Life insurance	$2.60

TOTAL DEDUCTIONS $217.65
NET PAY $662.35

1. What's Guy's gross pay?   ($880.00) $662.30

2. How much is Guy's state tax? $65.20 $104.15

3. How much is Guy's federal tax? $38.50 $104.15

4. How much are Guy's year-to-date earnings? $12,215.00 $880.00

2B. READ AND WRITE

Look at Guy's paycheck again. Answer the questions.

1. Who does Guy work for? _____ **Green River Parks Department** _____

2. Does Guy pay for life insurance? _____

3. Does Guy pay for health insurance? _____

4. When does the pay period end? _____

5. How many hours did Guy work? _____

6. Guy cashed this check at his bank. The bank didn't charge a fee.

   How much money did Guy get when he cashed this check? $ _____

Unit 7

hour	paycheck	payday	rate	start	time

A Anne, at Food Fair Supermarket, _____payday_____ is every Friday.

B Every Friday?

A Yes, you can pick up your _____ in the office.

B What's my pay _____?

A Your pay will start at $6.75 an _____. If you're on time every day in the week, you will get a $10 bonus that week.

B Good! I'm always on _____.

A Can you _____ work on Monday at 8:00?

B Yes, I can. Thanks.

3B. ANSWER THE QUESTIONS

Use the dialog in 3A.

1. When is payday at Food Fair Supermarket? _____every Friday_____

2. What is Anne's rate of pay? $_____ an hour

3. How much money will she get if she's on time every day? _____

4. Where can Anne get her paycheck? _____

5. When will Anne start her new job? _____

Unit 7

4. COMPLETE THE DIALOG

Human Resources	gross	~~mistake~~	wrong

A Alfredo, I think there's a _____ mistake _____ in my paycheck.

B What's _____ with it?

A Last week I worked 30 hours, so my _____ pay should be more.

B You're right. Check with _____ right away.

5. CIRCLE THE ANSWER

Read each statement about your paycheck. Circle the reason.

1. Overtime pay is added separately.

   a. The pay rate is different.

   b. Overtime is paid at the end of the year.

2. Your pay is less than usual.

   a. You worked fewer hours.

   b. Some money is lost.

3. Your health insurance deduction is more than usual.

   a. Someone in your workplace got sick.

   b. The cost of health insurance went up.

4. You don't get your paycheck.

   a. You weren't at work on payday.

   b. This month nobody gets a paycheck.

5. Your federal and state taxes are higher in this paycheck than in your last paycheck.

   a. You earned more this pay period.

   b. You worked fewer hours.

6. Your gross pay went up.

   a. You worked more hours.

   b. You were late a lot.

Unit 7

Complete the sentences.

Could you	look at my paycheck?
	answer a question?

1. _____Could you mail_____ (**mail**) my paycheck to my house this month?

2. _____ (**tell**) me how much my insurance deduction is?

3. _____ (**explain**) what federal tax is?

4. _____ (**repeat**) that information, please?

5. _____ (**show**) me how to figure out overtime pay?

6. _____ (**send**) me information about my health insurance?

7. _____ (**make**) a copy of this form?

6B. COMPLETE THE DIALOG

Use *could you* with the words in the box to complete the dialog.

call	~~explain~~	give	tell

A _____Could you explain_____ how to fill out tax forms in this country?

B I'll try.

A _____ me where to get tax forms?

B You can get them at the library and at government help centers.

A Is there a help center close to our workplace?

B Yes, there is. I have the address at home.

_____ me at home tonight?

A Sure. _____ me your phone number?

B Here it is.

A Thanks for the help.

Unit 7

6C. WRITE

Complete the sentences with *because* or *so*.

> I need to talk to my supervisor because I want to go on vacation.
> I want to go on vacation, so I need to talk to my supervisor.

1. Maria is saving money _____**because**_____ she wants to buy a car.

2. She wants to save $50 a month, _____ she puts $50 into the bank on the first day of every month.

3. Maria wants to buy a car _____ she wants to drive to work.

4. She needs to get a second job to save more money, _____ she reads the help wanted ads in the newspaper every day.

5. She wants to buy a used car _____ used cars are cheaper than new cars.

6D. COMPLETE THE PARAGRAPH

Use *because* or *so*.

Marco wanted a new job _____ he wanted to earn more money. He

wanted to learn about different jobs in his company, _____ he talked

to his boss yesterday. Marco was a good worker, _____ his boss

helped him. His boss told him about a good job in the warehouse. Tomorrow he'll

go to Human Resources, _____ he can find out more about the job.

Unit 7

Social Security Helps Millions

Social Security is a government program. It helps many older people and people who can't work. Sometimes, Social Security helps families after the husband or wife dies. Social Security sends people a monthly check. The check helps them to pay rent, to buy food, and to pay for other important things.

Social Security money comes from taxes. Every month, the government deducts money from every worker's paycheck for Social Security. Everyone who has a job pays these taxes. Young and old workers, full time and part time workers all help pay for Social Security. Social Security helps millions of people live better.

Check everyone who pays Social Security taxes.

❏ **1.** a 60-year old waitress

❏ **2.** a part time housekeeper

❏ **3.** a 7-year old child

❏ **4.** a high school student with a job after school

❏ **5.** a mechanic on the night shift

❏ **6.** a 65-year old woman who stopped working last year

7B. WRITE

Complete the sentences with information from the article.

older people	~~government~~	check	taxes	food

1. The _____government_____ runs Social Security.

2. Social Security helps many _____.

3. People who receive Social Security often get a _____ every month.

4. Workers in the U.S. pay _____ for Social Security.

5. Money from Social Security helps people pay for _____ .

Unit 7

Read the W-2 form. Read the questions. Circle the answers.

Employer's identification number		Wages, tips, other compensation	Federal income tax withheld
06-7899879		$22,347.00	$2,921.00
Employer's name , address, and zip code		Social Security Wages	Social Security tax withheld
Home Hardware 2345 Main Street Gainesville, FL 02340			$1,466.00
		Medicare wages and tips $22,347.00	Medicare tax withheld $362.55
Employee's Social Security number			
000-45-0922			
Employee's name , address, and zip code			
Ana Cheng 33457 South 122nd Gainesville, FL 02341			

Name of State	State wages, tips, etc.	State income tax		
FL	$22,347.00			

FORM W-2 Wages and Tax Statement **2000**

1. Whose W-2 form is it?   (Ana Cheng)   Gainesville, FL

2. Who is her employer?   Main Street Shopper   Home Hardware

3. What year is the form for?   2000   2010

4. How much were her wages? $22,347.00 $2,921.00

5. How much was her federal income tax? $362.55 $2,921.00

6. What does a W-2 form show?   wages and taxes   number of hours worked

9. THINK ABOUT YOUR LEARNING

Check the skills you learned in this unit.

❏ 1. Understand a paycheck.

❏ 2. Report mistakes in my paycheck.

❏ 3. Understand information about Social Security.

❏ 4. Understand a W-2 form.

Look at the skills you checked.
Which ones can help you at work? Write the numbers. _____

Health and Safety

1A. CIRCLE

Look at the pictures. Read the sentences. Circle *yes* or *no*.

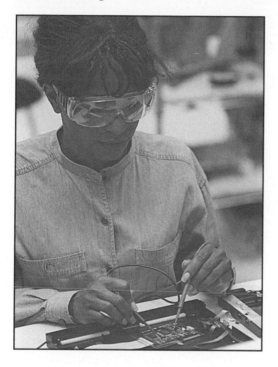

1. She's wearing a hard hat.

   yes (no)

2. She's wearing safety glasses.

   yes   no

3. She's wearing gloves.   yes   no

4. They're wearing safety glasses.

   yes   no

5. They're wearing hard hats.

   yes   no

6. They're wearing gloves.   yes   no

1B. WRITE

Write the safety clothes or equipment that you see at your workplace
or other workplaces.

1. _____

2. _____

3. _____

4. _____

5. _____

Look at the pictures. What are the people wearing?

| boots | ~~ear protection~~ | gloves | hard hat | hairnet | safety glasses |

1. _ear protection_

2. _____

3. _____

4. _____

5. _____

6. _____

2B. WRITE

Complete the chart. Write the safety equipment from 2A.
Write the part of the body each piece of safety equipment is for.

| head | feet | hands | ~~ears~~ | hair | eyes |

	Equipment	Part of the Body
1.	ear protection	ears
2.		
3.		
4.		
5.		
6.		

Unit 8

3A. WRITE

Look at the pictures. What should the people do?
Use the words in the box to write sentences.

| clean up | put on safety glasses | put on hard hats | get a fan |

1

They should put on safety glasses.

2

_____

3

_____

4

_____

3B. READ AND WRITE

What should you do to stay safe at your workplace? Check the boxes.
Add two ideas of your own.

❏ **1.** I should wear a hard hat.

❏ **2.** I should wear safety glasses.

❏ **3.** I should use ear protection.

❏ **4.** I should turn on the fan.

❏ **5.** I should _____.

❏ **6.** I should _____.

4A. WRITE

Look at the pictures. Warn people about the unsafe situations.

Excuse me. There's gas on the floor.

The gas can is leaking.

4B. WRITE

Look at Exercise 4A again. What should people do about the problems?
Write sentences.

1. _____ Put the gas in another gas can. _____

2. _____

3. _____

4. _____

What rules do the people need to follow? Write the number of the rule.

All package handlers for Overnight Package Express should follow these rules.

1. Wear a back support belt.
2. Wear safety shoes.
3. Wear ear protection when loading or unloading airplanes.
4. Wear your official orange uniform shirt or jacket when working around airplanes so that drivers and pilots can see you.

---

1. Tim wore sneakers to work. ___2___

2. Donna wore a pretty pink sweatshirt to stay warm while unloading a plane. _____

3. Mark listened to his radio while unloading a plane. _____

4. David always unloads planes. Today he left his back support belt at home. _____

Look at Exercise 5 again. Write *should* or *shouldn't*.

You	should	wear long sleeves.
	shouldn't	

1. Tim ___shouldn't___ wear sneakers to work.

2. Donna _____ wear her uniform shirt or jacket while unloading planes.

3. Mark _____ listen to the radio while unloading planes.

4. Mark _____ wear ear protection while unloading planes.

5. David _____ leave his back support belt at home.

6. David _____ wear his back support belt.

Write the letter.

> If she goes into the factory, she should wear a hard hat.
> She should wear a hard hat if she goes into the factory.

1. You should wear gloves ___b___.

2. If you work around very

   noisy machines, _____.

3. You should wear a hard hat _____.

4. If you lift heavy things, _____.

5. If you get a bad cut, _____.

a. you should wear a back support belt

~~b.~~ if you work with food

c. if you work at a construction site

d. you should wear ear protection

e. you should go to the hospital

7A. READ THE SAFETY INSTRUCTIONS

Which rule is Mary following? Write the number.

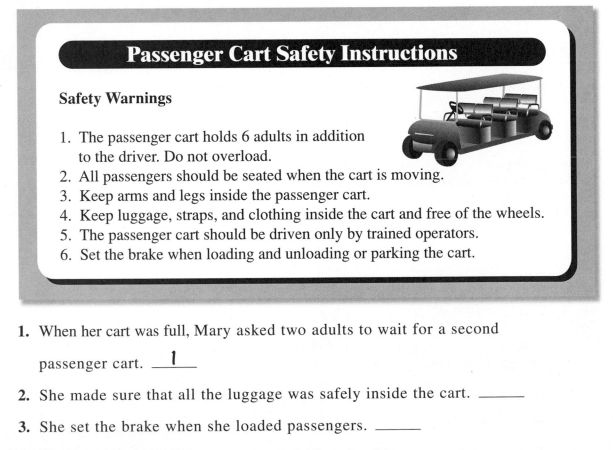

Passenger Cart Safety Instructions

Safety Warnings

1. The passenger cart holds 6 adults in addition to the driver. Do not overload.
2. All passengers should be seated when the cart is moving.
3. Keep arms and legs inside the passenger cart.
4. Keep luggage, straps, and clothing inside the cart and free of the wheels.
5. The passenger cart should be driven only by trained operators.
6. Set the brake when loading and unloading or parking the cart.

1. When her cart was full, Mary asked two adults to wait for a second

   passenger cart. ___1___

2. She made sure that all the luggage was safely inside the cart. _____

3. She set the brake when she loaded passengers. _____

4. She asked two children to sit down during the ride. _____

5. Mary is a trained operator. _____

Unit 8

Look at the picture. Complete the accident report.
Use today's date and the time now.

boss	box	hospital	~~room~~	shelf	towel

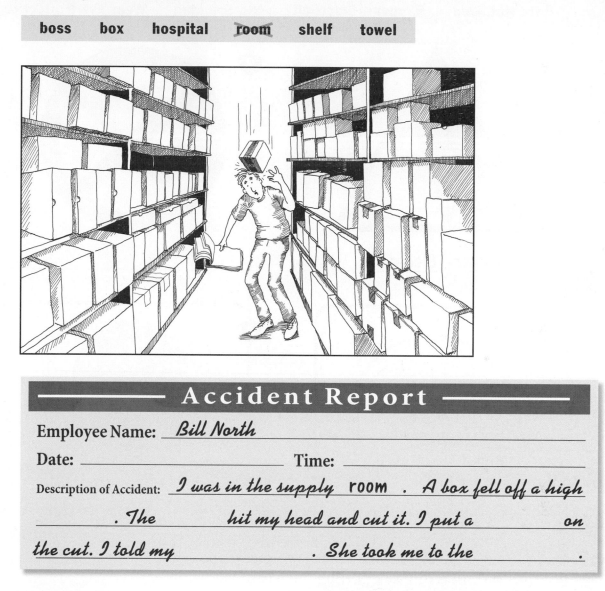

Accident Report

Employee Name: _Bill North_

Date: _____ Time: _____

Description of Accident: _I was in the supply_ room . _A box fell off a high_

_____ . The _____ hit my head and cut it. I put a_ _____ on

the cut. I told my _____ . She took me to the _____ .

7C. WRITE

What information is usually in an accident report?

1. _____**employee name**_____

2. _____

3. _____

4. _____

8. WRITE

Look at the signs. What do they mean? Write the warnings.

| Hard Hat Area | Danger – Electricity | No Smoking | Wear Eye Protection |

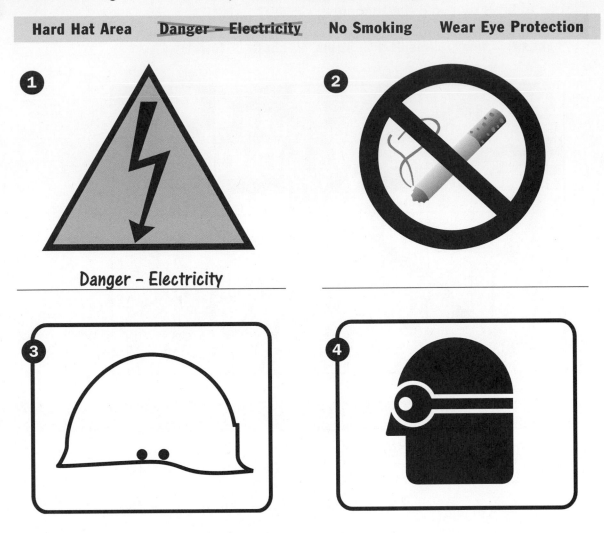

1 Danger – Electricity

2 _____

3 _____

4 _____

9. THINK ABOUT YOUR LEARNING

Check the skills you learned in this unit.

❑ **1.** Understand safety instructions.

❑ **2.** Follow safety instructions.

❑ **3.** Complete an accident report.

❑ **4.** Report unsafe situations.

Look at the skills you checked.
Which ones can help you at work? Write the numbers. _____

Working with People

1A. CIRCLE

Look at the picture. Answer the questions.

1. What are the people doing?

   (attending a meeting)   serving food to customers

2. Why is one person raising his hand?

   He wants to say something.   He wants to leave.

3. Why is one person standing up?

   She's in charge of the meeting.   She arrived late.

4. What do you think they are talking about?

   new products   computers

1B. CHECK

Check the things that you do at meetings. Add two more things.

❏ listen   ❏ ask questions

❏ raise my hand   ❏ _____

❏ talk   ❏ _____

Unit 9

Maintenance Department Employee Meeting

Topic: **New Cleaning Products**   Date: **August 3**
Time: **2:00 – 2:30**   Place: **Break Room**

2:00 – 2:15   Look at 4 new cleaning products
2:15 – 2:25   Gloves and safety glasses
2:25 – 2:30   Questions and answers

1. What day's the meeting? _____ August 3 _____

2. What time's the meeting? _____

3. Where's the meeting? _____

4. What's the topic of the meeting? _____

2B. WRITE

Look at the agenda. What information is usually part of an agenda?

1. _____ schedule _____

2. _____

3. _____

4. _____

5. _____

2C. THINK AND ANSWER

Think of a meeting you've been to. Answer the questions. Remember, meetings happen in towns and neighborhoods, sports clubs, and schools as well as at work.

1. What was the topic of the meeting? _____

2. Was there an agenda? _____

   What information was in it? _____

3. Did people talk about other things as well as the main topic? _____

   What did they talk about? _____

   _____

3A. COMPLETE THE DIALOG

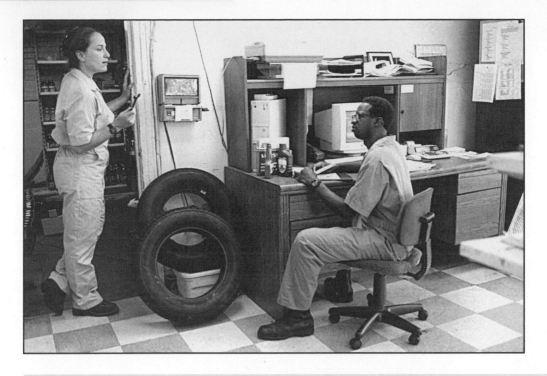

| agenda | ~~Can~~ | information | meeting | questions | Of course |

A Pardon me, Mr. Williams. _____ Can _____ we discuss Tuesday's meeting?

B _____, Carol.

A Several workers have _____ about the new health plan.

B Thank you for telling me. I'll put that on the _____. Is there anything else?

A Yes, could you give us more _____ about the vacation schedule?

B No problem. I'll bring copies to the _____.

3B. WRITE

What do you and your coworkers discuss? Write about topics you want to talk about at work or school.

1. _____ child care _____

2. _____

3. _____

4. _____

Unit 9

4. COMPLETE THE DIALOG

Complete the first sentence in each dialog.
Then write the policy at your workplace or school.

ask a question

Is there time for

~~have a question~~

1. A Excuse me. I _____ *have a question* _____ .

B Go ahead.

A Can we smoke only in the smoking area near the parking lot?

B _____ *That's right. Smoking is not allowed in the building.* _____

2. A Can I _____ ?

B Yes.

A Can I wear high heels to work?

B _____

3. A _____ one more question?

B Yes.

A Do I have to wear work boots every day?

B _____

5. READ AND ANSWER

Read the dialog. Answer the questions below.

Head Nurse: Our meeting today is about New Year's Eve.
December 31 is always a busy night in the hospital.

Ronny: Excuse me. Do we have to work extra hours that night?

Head Nurse: If you can work extra hours, that would be helpful.
We need to be organized and ready.

Sarah: Can I talk about the new weekend schedule?

Head Nurse: We'll talk about that later, Sarah. Let's get back to New Year's Eve.

1. What is the meeting about? _____ *New Year's Eve* _____

2. What does Ronny ask about? _____

3. Is Ronny's question related to the topic of the meeting? _____

4. What does Sarah ask about? _____

5. Is Sarah's question related to the topic of the meeting? _____

Unit 9

Complete the sentences using *have to* or *has to*.

I We You They	have to go to a meeting.	He She	has to go to a meeting.

1. She ____**has to**____ file papers.

2. You _____ go to the post office.

3. I _____ buy gas for the company van.

4. Bill _____ water the plants.

5. Maria and I _____ get more floor tiles.

6. Tim _____ deliver an order to a new customer.

7. She _____ clean the supply room.

8. Mark and Shelley _____ take a training class.

9. I _____ attend a meeting at 10:00.

6B. WRITE

Your work area or classroom needs cleaning. What do you have to do?
Write two sentences. Use *have to* or *has to*.

_____*I have to file these papers.*_____

_____

_____

6C. ANSWER THE QUESTIONS

1. What time do you have to go to work?

_____

2. What time do you have to go to school?

_____

3. What do you have to do on Saturday?

_____

6D. MATCH

Look at the pictures. Match the picture with the request.

I'd He'd She'd	like to ask about our vacation time.

We'd You'd They'd	like to ask about our vacation time.

a. I'd like to ask a question.

b. I'd like to start the meeting.

c. I'd like to return this suit.

d. I'd like you to change the tire.

6E. WRITE

We need to work faster because our customers want good service.
Our customers want good service, so we need to work faster.

Use *because* or *so* to complete the sentences.

1. I had a question about overtime pay, _____*so*_____ I asked my boss.

2. I have a meeting at 12:30, _____ I have to eat lunch quickly.

3. John can't come to work today _____ he's sick.

4. Mary got a promotion _____ she worked hard last year.

5. Ellen had several questions, _____ she talked to her boss.

6. I needed some paper clips, _____ I went to the supply room.

70

Unit 9

Mohammed is a welder. Read his questions.

a.	Where can I get a parking pass?
b.	Where are the supply request forms?
c.	Do we need a manager's signature to bring equipment to the repair center?
d.	Where are the new repair request forms?
e.	What time does the locker room close?
f.	Can we call to check on repairs?

Read the meeting agenda. Which of Mohammed's questions relate to the topic of this meeting? Which are not related? Write the letters in the lists below.

Meeting Agenda

Meeting for all Welders and Machinists

Topic: Repairs
Date: Friday, September 14
Time: 2:30
Place: Factory Meeting Room

Related to the Topic	Not Related to the Topic
_____	__a__
_____	_____
_____	_____

7B. WRITE

You're attending the meeting about the new system for requesting repairs. Write one or two questions you would ask.

Who should sign the repair request forms?

_____

_____

Read the article. Then read what Elena does to participate in meetings.
What should she do? Write *yes* or *no*.

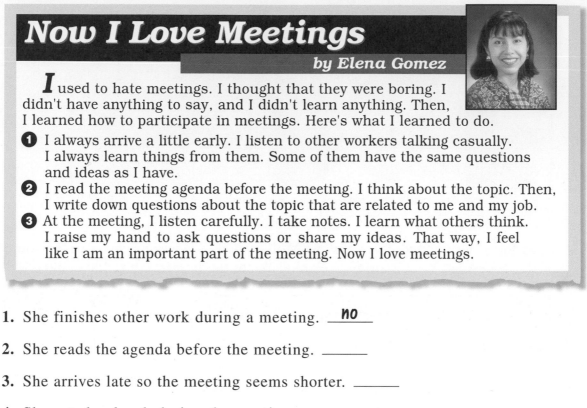

Now I Love Meetings
by Elena Gomez

I used to hate meetings. I thought that they were boring. I didn't have anything to say, and I didn't learn anything. Then, I learned how to participate in meetings. Here's what I learned to do.

❶ I always arrive a little early. I listen to other workers talking casually. I always learn things from them. Some of them have the same questions and ideas as I have.

❷ I read the meeting agenda before the meeting. I think about the topic. Then, I write down questions about the topic that are related to me and my job.

❸ At the meeting, I listen carefully. I take notes. I learn what others think. I raise my hand to ask questions or share my ideas. That way, I feel like I am an important part of the meeting. Now I love meetings.

1. She finishes other work during a meeting. __no__

2. She reads the agenda before the meeting. _____

3. She arrives late so the meeting seems shorter. _____

4. She eats her lunch during the meeting. _____

5. She thinks about the topic before the meeting. _____

6. She listens carefully and shares her ideas. _____

7. She takes notes during the meeting. _____

8. She asks questions during the meeting. _____

9. THINK ABOUT YOUR LEARNING

Check the skills you learned in this unit.

❏ 1. Understand an agenda.

❏ 2. Prepare for a meeting.

❏ 3. Ask questions in a meeting.

❏ 4. Make meetings work for me.

Look at the skills you checked.
Which ones can help you at work? Write the numbers. _____

UNIT ◆ 10 ◆ Career Development

1A. WRITE

Look at the picture. Answer the questions *yes* or *no*.

1. She's reading the newspaper. _____**yes**_____

2. She's looking for a new job. _____

3. She's at an interview. _____

4. She has paper and a pen to take notes. _____

5. She circled some of the advertisements. _____

1B. WRITE

Think about a job you applied for. Answer the questions.

1. Did you fill out a job application? _____

   Was it long or short? _____

2. Did you have an interview? _____

   How long was it? _____

3. What did you wear to the interview? _____

4. Where did you learn about the job opening? _____

Unit 10

73

If you are looking for a job, it's a good idea to list your strengths: your education, skills, and training. Write eight of your strengths.

	My Strengths
a.	
b.	
c.	
d.	
e.	
f.	
g.	
h.	

2B. MATCH

Look at the strengths you listed in 2A. Where do you write each one on a job application? Write the letters on the lines.

Employment Application

Personal Information

_____ **Education and Training**

_____ **Employment Record**

_____ **Other Skills and Qualifications**

3A. COMPLETE THE DIALOG

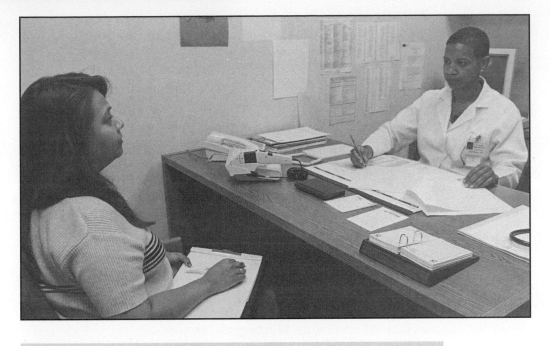

| helped | leave | long | wanted | ~~worked~~ | years |

A What did you do at your last job?

B I _____**worked**_____ at a nursing home.

A What did you do there?

B I served meals, changed sheets, and _____ the nurses.

A How _____ did you work at the nursing home?

B I worked there for two _____.

A Why did you _____ that job?

B I _____ to go to nursing school.

3B. WRITE

Answer the questions.

1. What did you do at your last job? _____

_____

2. How long were you at that job? _____

3. Why did you leave that job? _____

_____

4. WRITE

Think about these interview questions. Write answers you might give.
Use the answers in the box or write your own.

| Yes, I have experience doing that. | No, but I'm a fast learner. |

1. Can you stock shelves? _____ *Yes, I have experience doing that.* _____

2. Can you use a cash register? _____

3. Did you work with customers in your last job? _____

4. Can you take telephone messages? _____

5. Can you organize and file papers? _____

5A. READ AND CIRCLE

Read the letter. Then circle the reasons Marco got the job.

★ Star Welding Company Carlsbad, New Mexico 87654

Dear Mr. Hernandez,

Thank you for applying to Star Welding Company. We were very
impressed with your work experience. Also, your past employers
gave you excellent recommendations.

We would like to offer you a position with our company.
Please call 555-9987 to discuss this offer.

1. He has special training.   2. He knows the company manager.

3. He has experience.   4. He has good recommendations.

5B. CIRCLE

What are some reasons people do not get jobs? Circle the numbers.
Add two ideas of your own.

1. They don't have the right training.   2. They don't have the right experience.

3. They're always early to work.   4. They got a good education.

5. They were late to the interview.   6. _____

7. _____

6A. COMPLETE THE DIALOG

Did	you	work in a factory?		Yes,	I	did.
	they			No,		didn't.

A _____Did_____ you _____work_____ (work) in a restaurant?

B No, I _____didn't_____. I _____worked_____ (work) in a canning factory.

A _____ you _____ (follow) the health rules?

B Yes, I _____. I _____ (wash) my hands, and I _____ (use) a hairnet and gloves.

A _____ you _____ (open) clams?

B Yes, I _____. I _____ (open) them with a knife, and I took out the meat.

A _____ you _____ (cook) the meat?

B No, I _____. I _____ (check) the meat for quality.

A _____ you _____ (add) anything to the meat?

B Yes, I _____. I _____ (add) salt and water.

Unit 10

6B. WRITE

Complete the paragraph.

I	drove didn't drive	a van.

Irregular Verbs			
carry	carried	make	made
drive	drove	put	put
give	gave	run	ran
go	went	take	took
have	had	write	wrote

Shirley wants to be an electrician. She is taking classes at City Technical

College. Shirley _____**had**_____ (**have**) a lot of homework last night.

She _____ (**write**) a report on safety rules for electricians.

Shirley _____ (**go**) to school today after work. Shirley

_____ (**not drive**). She _____ (**take**) the

bus. The bus was late, so she _____ (**run**) to class. She

_____ (**not want**) to be late. She _____

(**give**) her report to the class. The class _____ (**take**) notes on

her report. After school, she _____ (**go**) home.

6C. COMPLETE THE SENTENCES

Carlos had a job interview yesterday. Write the correct form of the word.

I	learn quickly. answer politely.

1. Carlos dressed _____**neatly**_____ (**neat**).

2. He smiled _____ (**nice**).

3. He said, "I can learn _____ (**quick**)."

4. He said, "I always work _____ (**careful**)."

5. He asked questions _____ (**polite**).

6. The interviewer answered Carlos' questions

_____ (**patient**).

Unit 10

7A. READ AND WRITE

Circle the answers about the job announcement.

WALKER ELECTRONIC GOODS

Assemblers Needed

Walker Electronic Goods needs
a F/T assembler. No exp. nec.
Pos. avail. immediately. Excl. bnfts.
Call Judy at 555-0097

1. What job is advertised?   salesperson   (assembler)

2. Is experience needed?   yes   no

3. Is the job full time or part time?   full time   part time

4. When does the job begin?   next month   now

5. What is offered?   high pay   good benefits

6. How should you apply?   go to the factory   call Judy

7B. WRITE

Apply for a job you want. Complete the application.

Application for Employment

Date _____ Job you are applying for _____

Name _____
             Last   First

Address _____

_____

Social Security Number _____ Telephone _____

Work History

Last Company _____ Job _____

Telephone _____ How long were you at this job? _____

_____   _____
Signature   Date

Read the article. Answer the questions. Write *yes* or *no*.

INTERVIEW POWER

How can you prepare for an interview?

The interviewer will probably ask you about your work experience, skills, and training. He or she also may ask what you know about the company. You should prepare your answers before the interview.

Let's say you are interviewing for a job as a painter. The interviewer will probably ask you, "Do you have experience as a painter?" Be ready to answer, even if you only have a little experience. You might answer, "I painted my neighbor's kitchen. And I painted my friend's house. I can learn quickly."

Before your interview, find out about the business. What do they paint? How many employees do they have?

Remember that employers are looking for people who are excited about the job. They are looking for people who are interested in the work. So be sure you bring excitement and interest to your interview. It may be the most important thing you do!

1. You should learn about the company where you are applying. ____**yes**____

2. You should show excitement about the job. _____

3. Your clothes are the most important part of your interview. _____

4. You should prepare your answers before the interview. _____

5. If you don't have experience, it's OK to say that you do. _____

6. If you don't have much experience, you can say that you learn quickly. _____

9. THINK ABOUT YOUR LEARNING

Check the skills you learned in this unit.

❏ **1.** Look for a job.

❏ **2.** Interview for a job.

❏ **3.** Understand hiring decisions.

❏ **4.** Complete a job application.

Look at the skills you checked.
Which ones can help you at work? Write the numbers. _____

Unit 10

Answer Key

Exercise 1A (page 1)
1. yes
2. yes
3. no
4. no

Exercise 1B (page 1)
Many answers are possible. Share your answers with another learner or your teacher.

Exercise 2A (page 2)
1. help
2. is
3. call
4. May
5. This

Exercise 2B (page 2)
Many answers are possible but may include the following:
Security. Nadia Petrov.
Security. This is Nadia Petrov.
Security. How can I help you?
Security. This is Nadia Petrov. May I help you?
This is Security. Nadia Petrov speaking.

Exercise 2C (page 2)
Many answers are possible. Share your answers with another learner or your teacher.

Exercise 3A (page 3)
1. 555-8585
2. 555-9855
3. 781-555-0087

Exercise 3B (page 3)
Many answers are possible but should include one of the following names and corresponding telephone numbers with the information in the proper sequence:
Joseph Miguel, 555-8934
Morris Office Supplies, 555-9855
Laura Murray, 781-555-0087
Dr. Anita Thomas, 555-8585
Athletic Technology Corporation, 555-3390

Exercise 3C (page 3)
Many answers are possible. Share your answers with another learner or your teacher.

Exercise 4 (page 4)
These words should be crossed out:
age   drink   telephone number
date   dessert   job
time   country

Exercise 5A (page 4)
1. Jack Morales
2. about 10:00
3. tape and large paper clips
4. Thursday/today
5. *Many answers are possible but may include the following:*
   Yes, he gave all the information.
   No, he didn't leave his telephone number.

Exercise 5B (page 4)
Many answers are possible. Share your answers with another learner or your teacher.

Exercise 6A (page 5)
1. 'm
2. 's
3. 're
4. 's

Exercise 6B (page 5)
1. opens
2. answer
3. help
4. writes
5. work

Exercise 6C (page 6)
1. have
2. has
3. have
4. has
5. have
6. has

Exercise 6D (page 6)
1. her
2. me
3. them
4. him
5. her

Exercise 7 (page 7)

```
For  Carolina
Date  Answers will vary.  Time
      While You Were Out
From  David Salinas
Of  Sales
Phone  2990

  TELEPHONED       CAME TO SEE YOU
  PLEASE CALL      WILL CALL AGAIN

MESSAGE _____
_____
_____
_____

SIGNED  Samuel
```

Exercise 8 (page 8)
1. Chen Lee, 555-8962
2. Bettina Rios *or*
   The Lunch Box, 555-0899
3. Marty Morris *or*
   Regal Window Cleaners, 555-9811

Exercise 9 (page 8)
Many answers are possible. Share your answers with another learner or your teacher.

U N I T 2

Exercise 1A (page 9)
1. yes
2. no
3. yes
4. no
5. yes

Exercise 1B (page 9)
Many answers are possible. Share your answers with another learner or your teacher.

Exercise 2A (page 10)
1. pen
2. stapler
3. scissors
4. file cabinet
5. lawn mower
6. hand truck
7. ladder
8. hammer

Exercise 2B (page 10)
1. ladder
2. hand truck
3. lawn mower
4. hammer
5. file cabinet
6. scissors

Exercise 3 (page 11)
1. top
2. middle
3. bottom
4. bottom
5. middle
6. top
7. middle

Exercise 4 (page 12)
Check: paper clips, pencils, rubber bands, staples

Exercise 5 (page 12)
1. d
2. c
3. a
4. b

Exercise 6A (page 13)
1. A Are there light bulbs?
   B Yes, there are.
2. A Is there a ladder?
   B Yes, there is.

3. A Are there bulletin boards?
   B Yes, there are.
4. A Is there a lawn mower?
   B No, there isn't.

5. A Is there a cart?
   B Yes, there is.
6. A Are there rubber bands?
   B No, there aren't.

7.　A　Is there a hammer?
　　B　No, there isn't.
8.　A　Is there a copier?
　　B　No, there isn't.

Exercise 6B (page 13)
A　any
B　some, some
A　any
B　some, any

Exercise 6C (page 14)
1.　on top of
2.　under
3.　on top of
4.　behind
5.　against

Exercise 7A (page 15)
Bills　a, d, g
Resume　c
Instruction Books　b, e, f

Exercise 7B (page 15)
Many answers are possible but may include the following:
1.　Resumes
2.　Instruction Books
3.　Repair Requests

Exercise 8 (page 16)
1.　b
2.　d
3.　e
4.　c
5.　a
6.　f

Exercise 9 (page 16)
Many answers are possible. Share your answers with another learner or your teacher.

U N I T ◆3

Exercise 1A (page 17)
1.　c
2.　d
3.　a
4.　b

Exercise 1B (page 17)
Many answers are possible. Share your answers with another learner or your teacher.

Exercise 2A (page 18)
1.　tire
2.　cash register
3.　microwave oven
4.　lawn mower
5.　van
6.　oil

Exercise 2B (page 18)
Many answers are possible. Share your answers with another learner or your teacher.

Exercise 2C (page 18)
Many answers are possible. Share your answers with another learner or your teacher.

Exercise 3A (page 19)
A　broken
B　ask, fix
A　department
B　say
A　maintenance

Exercise 3B (page 19)
Many answers are possible. Share your answers with another learner or your teacher.

Exercise 4 (page 20)
Sentences will vary but should be similar to the following:
1.　He put his coffee on the computer.
2.　He didn't clean the microwave oven.
3.　She put a lot of soap in the dishwasher.
4.　He didn't put air in the tire.

Exercise 5 (page 20)
1.　October 25
2.　the company van
3.　He changed a flat tire.
4.　Arturo Diaz

Exercise 6A (page 21)
1.　fixed
2.　didn't clean
3.　checked
4.　didn't sharpen
5.　didn't change

Exercise 6B (page 21)
1.　Marta delivered the package to Mr. Brown.
2.　She cleaned the kitchen in the break room.

3. She didn't help Joyce organize the supply room.
4. She didn't repair the cash register.
5. She didn't fix the coffee maker.

Exercise 6C (page 22)
A   Did, work
B   finished
A   Did, like
B   did, liked
A   Did, start
B   did, started
A   Did, talk
B   didn't, talked

Exercise 6D (page 22)
1. sent
2. didn't send
3. bought
4. took
5. went
6. had

Exercise 7A (page 23)

VALLEY HOTEL SERVICE REQUEST	
Name:	Kim Lee
Date:	March 17
Equipment:	lamp
Description:	The floor lamp in room 122 doesn't work. The switch is broken.
For service technician only: SERVICE CODE	009

VALLEY HOTEL SERVICE REQUEST	
Name:	Joel Prevalus
Date:	March 28
Equipment:	carpet
Description:	The carpet in room 111 has a large worn spot in front of the door. It needs to be replaced.
For service technician only: SERVICE CODE	052

Exercise 7B (page 23)

VALLEY HOTEL SERVICE REQUEST	
Name:	(your name)
Date:	(today's date)
Equipment:	clock
Description:	*Answers may vary but should include:* The clock in the break room doesn't work. It needs to be fixed.

Exercise 8 (page 24)
1. b
2. a
3. d
4. c
5. g

Exercise 9 (page 24)
Many answers are possible. Share your answers with another learner or your teacher.

UNIT 4

Exercise 1A (page 25)
1. yes
2. no
3. yes
4. no
5. yes

Exercise 1B (page 25)
Many answers are possible. Share your answers with another learner or your teacher.

Exercise 2A (page 26)
B   meeting
A   sorry, about
B   How
A   free

Exercise 2B (page 26)
Written on calendar on Tuesday, July 14: City Computer Company, 10:00-4:00.

Exercise 2C (page 26)
Written on calendar in 2B on Thursday, July 16: Big Mountain Skis, 9:00-7:00.

Exercise 3 (page 27)
1. 7:00
2. 8:00
3. no
4. yes

Exercise 4 (page 27)
1. Thursday, May 14
2. 8:00
3. no
4. yes

Exercise 5A (page 28)
1. 200
2. January 23
3. 9:30 a.m.
4. 9:00 p.m.
5. 5

Exercise 5B (page 28)
9:00   Tim Young
10:00   Diane Johnson
11:00   Sunja Kim
12:00   Donna Diaz

Exercise 6A (page 29)

1. You have to punch in.
2. They have to go to meetings.
3. We don't have to work on weekends.
4. She has to work with a team.
5. He doesn't have to wear a uniform.

Exercise 6B (page 29)

A   Do, have to clean
B   have to clean
A   Do, have to wash
B   don't have to wash, have to wash
A   Do, have to make
B   have to make

Exercise 6C (page 30)

Sentences will vary but may include the following:

1. He's going to sort overnight packages from 8:30 to 9:00.
2. He's going to deliver packages to the departments from 9:00 to 10:00.
3. He's going to prepare outgoing packages from 10:00 to 11:00.
4. He's going to eat lunch from 12:00 to 1:00.
5. He's going to sort mail from 1:00 to 2:00.
6. He's going to deliver mail from 2:00 to 4:00.

Exercise 6D (page 30)

Many answers are possible. Share your answers with another learner or your teacher.

Exercise 7A (page 31)

Circled Tasks:
Deliver the new cash registers to the North Mall store
Deliver holiday decorations to the North Mall store

Underlined Tasks:
Get a ladder from the warehouse
Meet the new warehouse manager at the warehouse
Return tools to the warehouse

Exercise 7B (page 31)

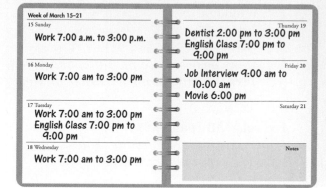

Exercise 8 (page 32)

1. yes
2. no
3. Thursday, November 28
4. 11:30 am

Exercise 9 (page 32)

Many answers are possible. Share your answers with another learner or your teacher.

U N I T 5

Exercise 1A (page 33)

1. c
2. d
3. a
4. b

Exercise 1B (page 33)

Many answers are possible. Share your answers with another learner or your teacher.

Exercise 2A (page 34)

A   refund
B   credit
A   Can
B   show

Exercise 2B (page 34)

Many answers are possible but should be similar to the following:

1. I'm sorry. I need to check that with my supervisor
2. Of course. I'd be happy to help.
3. I'm sorry. I can't. I already have plans. Did you ask Donna?
4. Certainly. I can help you right now.

Exercise 3A (page 35)

1. Why don't
2. Let's
3. Why not
4. *Many answers are possible. Share your answers with another learner or your teacher.*

Exercise 3B (page 35)

Many answers are possible. Share your answers with another learner or your teacher.

Exercise 4 (page 36)

1. c
2. a
3. d
4. b

Exercise 5 (page 36)

1. an office
2. a taxi
3. a city street

Exercise 6A (page 37)

1. A Where   B bought
2. A When   B saw
3. A Where   B found
4. A How   B got
5. A When   B made

Exercise 6B (page 37)

Many answers are possible. Share your answers with another learner or your teacher.

Exercise 6C (page 38)

A Did, check   B did
A Did, check   B did
A Did, change   B didn't
A Did, change   B did
A Did, put   B didn't

Exercise 7A (page 38 and 39)

1. yes
2. no
3. yes
4. yes
5. yes

Exercise 7B (page 39)

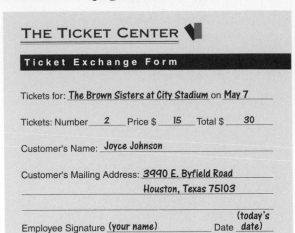

THE TICKET CENTER

Ticket Exchange Form

Tickets for: <u>The Brown Sisters at City Stadium</u> on <u>May 7</u>

Tickets: Number ___2___ Price $ ___15___ Total $ ___30___

Customer's Name: <u>Joyce Johnson</u>

Customer's Mailing Address: <u>3990 E. Byfield Road</u>
<u>Houston, Texas 75103</u>

Employee Signature <u>(your name)</u>   Date <u>(today's date)</u>

Exercise 8 (page 40)

1. b
2. a
3. a
4. b

Exercise 9 (page 40)

Many answers are possible. Share your answers with another learner or your teacher.

U N I T  6

Exercise 1A (page 41)

Circle: 1, 2, 4, and 5.

Exercise 1B (page 41)

Many answers are possible. Share your answers with another learner or your teacher.

Exercise 2A (page 42)

1. c
2. a
3. b

Exercise 2B (page 42)

Many answers are possible. Share your answers with another learner or your teacher.

Exercise 3A (page 43)

A Excuse, Can
B sorry
A can't
B off
A idea

Exercise 3B (page 43)

Many answers are possible. Share your answers with another learner or your teacher.

Exercise 4A (page 44)
1. c
2. a
3. b

Exercise 4B (page 44)

Many answers are possible but may include the following:

Excuse me. Could you please turn down your music?

Excuse me. It's a little loud at my desk. Could you turn off your radio?

Exercise 5A (page 45)

Many answers are possible but may include checks for the following items:

She gets to work on time.
She does good work.
She works hard.
She's helpful to others.
She's friendly.
She's cooperative.
She's very careful.
She follows the safety rules.

Exercise 5B (page 45)

Many answers are possible. Share your answers with another learner or your teacher.

Exercise 6A (page 46)
1. smaller than
2. larger than
3. bigger than
4. longer than
5. cheaper than
6. uglier than
7. nicer than
8. worse than
9. tighter than
10. better than

Exercise 6B (page 47)
1. more practical than
2. more expensive than
3. more comfortable than
4. more attractive than

Exercise 7A (page 47)
1. no
2. no
3. no
4. no
5. yes

Exercise 7B (page 48)

Many answers are possible but may include the following:

Child care aides have to arrive on time.
Child care aides have to clean up at the end of the day.
Child care aides have to stay until the end of their shift.

Exercise 8 (page 48)

Circle: serve good food, serve food fast, have low prices.

Exercise 9 (page 48)

Many answers are possible. Share your answers with another learner or your teacher.

U N I T 7

Exercise 1A (page 49)
1. in a library
2. getting tax forms
3. to pay taxes

Exercise 1B (page 49)
1. *Many answers are possible but may include:* the last day of the month; every Friday; twice a month.
2. *Many answers are possible but may include:* some libraries, IRS offices.
3. *Many answers are possible. Share your answers with another learner or your teacher.*

Exercise 2A (page 50)
1. $880.00
2. $65.20
3. $104.15
4. $12,215.00

Exercise 2B (page 50)
1. Green River Parks Department
2. yes
3. no
4. 9-15-99
5. 80
6. $662.35

Exercise 3A (page 51)
A   payday
A   paycheck
B   rate
A   hour
B   time
A   start

Exercise 3B (page 51)
1.   every Friday
2. $6.75 an hour
3. $10 bonus for that week
4.   in the office
5.   Monday at 8:00

Exercise 4 (page 52)
A   mistake
B   wrong
A   gross
B   Human Resources

Exercise 5 (page 52)
1.   a
2.   a
3.   b
4.   a
5.   a
6.   a

Exercise 6A (page 53)
1.   Could you mail
2.   Could you tell
3.   Could you explain
4.   Could you repeat
5.   Could you show
6.   Could you send
7.   Could you make

Exercise 6B (page 53)
A   Could you explain
A   Could you tell
B   Could you call
A   Could you give

Exercise 6C (page 54)
1.   because
2.   so
3.   because
4.   so
5.   because

Exercise 6D (page 54)
because, so, so, so

Exercise 7A (page 55)
Check: 1, 2, 4, and 5.

Exercise 7B (page 55)
1.   government
2.   older people
3.   check
4.   taxes
5.   food

Exercise 8 (page 56)
1.   Ana Cheng
2.   Home Hardware
3.   2000
4. $22,347.00
5. $2,921.00
6.   wages and taxes

Exercise 9 (page 56)
Many answers are possible. Share your answers with another learner or your teacher.

<u>U N I T</u> ◆8◆

Exercise 1A (page 57)
1.   no
2.   yes
3.   no
4.   no
5.   yes
6.   yes

Exercise 1B (page 57)
Many answers are possible. Share your answers with another learner or your teacher.

Exercise 2A (page 58)
1.   ear protection
2.   hard hat
3.   boots
4.   hairnet
5.   safety glasses
6.   gloves

Exercise 2B (page 58)

1. ear protection   ears
2. hard hat   head
3. boots   feet
4. hairnet   hair
5. safety glasses   eyes
6. gloves   hands

Exercise 3A (page 59)

1. They should put on safety glasses.
2. They should get a fan.
3. They should put on hard hats.
4. They should clean up.

Exercise 3B (page 59)

Many answers are possible. Share your answers with another learner or your teacher.

Exercise 4A (page 60)

Many answers are possible but may include the following:
1. Excuse me. There's gas on the floor. The gas can is leaking.
2. Excuse me. There's water on the floor.
3. Excuse me. The ladder is right in front of that door.
4. Excuse me. There's broken glass by the pool.

Exercise 4B (page 60)

Many answers are possible but may include the following:
1. Put the gas in another gas can.
2. Mop up the water.
3. Move the ladder.
4. Clean up the broken glass.

Exercise 5 (page 61)

1. 2
2. 4
3. 3
4. 1

Exercise 6A (page 61)

1. shouldn't
2. should
3. shouldn't
4. should
5. shouldn't
6. should

Exercise 6B (page 62)

1. b
2. d
3. c
4. a
5. e

Exercise 7A (page 62)

1. 1
2. 4
3. 6
4. 2
5. 5

Exercise 7B (page 63)

———— Accident Report ————

Employee Name: *Bill North*

Date: _____*Answers will vary*_____   Time: _____*Answers will vary*_____

Description of Accident: *I was in the supply* room . *A box fell off a high*
shelf . *The* box *hit my head and cut it. I put a* towel on
the cut. I told my boss . *She took me to the* hospital .

Exercise 7C (page 63)

1. employee name
2. date
3. time
4. description of the accident

Exercise 8 (page 64)

1. Danger–Electricity
2. No Smoking
3. Hard Hat Area
4. Wear Eye Protection

Exercise 9 (page 64)

Many answers are possible. Share your answers with another learner or your teacher.

U N I T ◇9◇

Exercise 1A (page 65)

1. attending a meeting
2. He wants to say something.
3. She's in charge of the meeting.
4. new products

Exercise 1B (page 65)

Many answers are possible. Share your answers with another learner or your teacher.

Exercise 2A (page 66)
1. August 3
2. 2:00–2:30
3. Break Room
4. new cleaning products

Exercise 2B (page 66)
1. schedule
2. date
3. time
4. place
5. topic

Exercise 2C (page 66)
Many answers are possible. Share your answers with another learner or your teacher.

Exercise 3A (page 67)
A Can
B Of course
A questions
B agenda
A information
B meeting

Exercise 3B (page 67)
Many answers are possible. Share your answers with another learner or your teacher.

Exercise 4 (page 68)
1. A have a question
   B That's right. Smoking is not allowed in the building.
2. A ask a question
   B *Many answers are possible. Share your answers with another learner or your teacher.*
3. A Is there time for
   B *Many answers are possible. Share your answers with another learner or your teacher.*

Exercise 5 (page 68)
1. New Year's Eve
2. He asks if they have to work extra hours.
3. yes
4. She asks about the new weekend schedule.
5. no

Exercise 6A (page 69)
1. has to
2. have to
3. have to
4. has to
5. have to
6. has to
7. has to
8. have to
9. have to

Exercise 6B (page 69)
Many answers are possible. Share your answers with another learner or your teacher.

Exercise 6C (page 69)
Many answers are possible. Share your answers with another learner or your teacher.

Exercise 6D (page 70)
1. b
2. d
3. a
4. c

Exercise 6E (page 70)
1. so
2. so
3. because
4. because
5. so
6. so

Exercise 7A (page 71)
Related to the Topic: c, d, f
Not Related to the Topic: a, b, e

Exercise 7B (page 71)
Many answers are possible. Share your answers with another learner or your teacher.

Exercise 8 (page 72)
1. no
2. yes
3. no
4. no
5. yes
6. yes
7. yes
8. yes

Exercise 9 (page 72)
Many answers are possible. Share your answers with another learner or your teacher.

Exercise 1A (page 73)
1. yes
2. yes
3. no
4. yes
5. yes

Exercise 1B (page 73)
Many answers are possible. Share your answers with another learner or your teacher.

Exercise 2A (page 74)
Many answers are possible. Share your answers with another learner or your teacher.

Exercise 2B (page 74)
Many answers are possible. Share your answers with another learner or your teacher.

Exercise 3A (page 75)
B worked
B helped
A long
B years
A leave
B wanted

Exercise 3B (page 75)
Many answers are possible. Share your answers with another learner or your teacher.

Exercise 4 (page 76)
Many answers are possible. Share your answers with another learner or your teacher.

Exercise 5A (page 76)
Circle: 3 and 4.

Exercise 5B (page 76)
Circle: 1, 2, and 5.
Many answers are possible. Share your answers with another learner or your teacher.

Exercise 6A (page 77)
A Did, work
B didn't, worked
A Did, follow
B did, washed, used
A Did, open
B did, opened
A Did, cook
B didn't, checked
A Did, add
B did, added

Exercise 6B (page 78)
had, wrote, went, didn't drive, took, ran, didn't want, gave, took, went

Exercise 6C (page 78)
1. neatly
2. nicely
3. quickly
4. carefully
5. politely
6. patiently

Exercise 7A (page 79)
1. assembler
2. no
3. full time
4. now
5. good benefits
6. call Judy

Exercise 7B (page 79)
Many answers are possible. Share your answers with another learner or your teacher.

Exercise 8 (page 80)
1. yes
2. yes
3. no
4. yes
5. no
6. yes

Exercise 9 (page 80)
Many answers are possible. Share your answers with another learner or your teacher.